MEREDITH® BOOKS
DES MOINES, IOWA

Meredith Books
1716 Locust Street
Des Moines, Iowa 50309–3023
meredithbooks.com

Printed in the United States of America.

First Edition.
Library of Congress Control Number: 2007933385
ISBN: 978-0-696-23829-1

Culinary Consultants
Sonia D. Armstead, Rochelle Brown Johnson, Duane Maxwell

Photographers: Robert Jacobs, Blaine Moats

DEDICATION

I want to dedicate this book to two great people, my first true supporters, two men who gave me my first opportunities to work in real restaurant environments: Mr. Bernard Stricker and Mr. Joseph Legader.

Bernard Stricker gave me the chance to work in his restaurant, the Old Vinings Inn, in Atlanta when I was just 14 years old. Bernard Stricker taught me the proper use of a knife and the proper understanding of responsibility and discipline. He was a tough man but he always knew what he wanted. Trust and belief in myself are the best gifts he ever gave me. I know that I am able to write my second cookbook because he gave me a chance to change my life through food. My greatest appreciation goes to Mr. Bernard Stricker. I dedicate this book to you. Rest in peace.

Joseph Legader was the executive chef at The Ritz-Carlton, Atlanta and gave me my first chance to work not only in one of the best hotels in the country but in the gourmet dining room. For a young black male from the Atlanta projects, this was the opportunity of a lifetime. It meant more to me than anything you can imagine. Chef Legader taught me to truly understand food at a level that I had not known. I worked hard to fit into this new world of food and because of it I got the promotion that landed me near Palm Springs at The Ritz-Carlton, Rancho Mirage. Chef Joseph Legader, I dedicate this book to you. Thank you for believing in me.

THANKS AND ACKNOWLEDGMENTS

First I'd like to thank my incredible team at Power House Productions/Management—**Rochelle Brown** and **Sonia Armstead**. Also the great Power House staff: **Duane Maxwell, David Martin, Neman Walbe,** and **Joycelyn Williams**—for all their much-needed work and support in getting this book finished in a very short time.

A special thanks to my dear friend **Tobin Montgomery** for all his great consulting work on this book. To the entire staff at **TV One**, including **Demarco Kidd** and **Stacy Simmions**, for their continued support on my books and cooking shows. To **Sean Perry** and **Ivo Fisher** at **Endeavor Agency** for their great and much-needed advice. To Jacky Brander at Fred Segal Fun and her great team, including **Hope** and **TJ**. To the staff at **Meredith Books** for believing in me for the second time and supporting my new and exciting book career.

I'd like to take this opportunity to thank **every single person** who purchased my first book, *Turn Up the Heat with G. Garvin.* It's because of you that I am able to write and deliver this second book. Your support is truly a blessing, so thank you.

As always, I would like to thank **my family** for always being there to pick me up when I fall. I love you all. You know your names, so I don't need to tell you who you are. Your son, your brother, your uncle, your dad loves you all.

A very special thanks to my daughter **Nola Miltaly Garvin** for giving me a reason to keep going when I can't think of one. Thank you. And, as always, daddy really loves you!

GOOD TIMES
AND GOOD FOOD.
KEEPING IT
SIMPLE AND
KEEPING IT
SMOOTH——
THAT'S WHAT
*MAKE IT SUPER
SIMPLE* IS
ALL ABOUT.

CONTENTS

INTRODUCTION

My beautiful little girl is now age 4 going on 16. It's amazing how quickly little people change and in such big ways. Her sentences are complete (with a stutter or two), and she wants to—no, she insists on—dressing herself. It's absolutely impossible for me to make breakfast without her pulling up her chair to help. I crack the eggs; she mixes them. I put in the salt; she puts in the pepper. I cut the avocado; she lays out the turkey bacon—and together we're off to the races.

We don't often make it to the breakfast table. Instead we eat at the kitchen counter, gabbing about her two best friends Sasha and Houston and all that's going on in the lives of a couple of 4-year-olds. There's nothing like a conversation with a child who says she is no longer a baby and whose favorite questions are "Why?" and "But, why?" These are very special, very simple times. This is what I call life. This is what I live for. This is what I'm giving you in this book, *Make It Super Simple*.

"THESE ARE SOME OF MY BEST RECIPES EVER, AND BELIEVE YOU ME, IT DOESN'T GET ANY EASIER THAN THIS!"

It's really interesting to talk to people about food and cooking (or the lack thereof). No one has the time to cook, but everyone has the time to go out and eat.

But to me, eating out seems to take so much more time than fixing a meal at home. First you've got to shower, get dressed, then do your hair and figure out your clothes and shoes. You go to pick up your date, but she's not ready, so you wait. (It's OK that she's not ready, but you're still waiting.) Once she's ready, you drive 20 minutes to the restaurant, then you drive around another 15 minutes looking for parking because you don't want to do the valet thing for whatever the reason. Finally, you find a space blocks away and spend another 10 minutes walking to the restaurant. Of course at the restaurant, there's a small wait, so you order a drink and relax before dinner. After you finally sit down and order three or four courses and enjoy a bottle of wine, you've probably spent four or five hours going out to dinner. In the same amount of time, you could drive to Las Vegas (from Los Angeles) or fly to San Francisco twice. If you lived in Atlanta, you may as well fly to New York to eat. That seems to me more than enough time to cook a meal.

My goal for this book is to introduce cooking to anyone who never has tried cooking but wants to—and to reintroduce cooking to anyone who's cooked and enjoyed it but now can't find time to get into the kitchen. The focus here is cooking in a very simple way—the easy way.

Truth be told, some of us just don't have the time on a regular basis to prepare complicated recipes. There are still only 24 hours in a day. If eight are dedicated for sleep, eight to ten for work, and one to two hours for travel, you end up with six to eight hours. That time is quickly filled with homework (if you have kids), laundry, and picking up the house. This doesn't leave a lot of time to actually cook and enjoy a meal.

But great food doesn't have to mean complicated, just as success doesn't have to mean money.

Think of some of the simplest aspects of life—the air you breathe, a glass of water, the hand you hold while walking, the sound of the ocean at midnight, the power of a kiss from your daughter or son, talking on the phone with a friend, and the joy of opening up your eyes in the morning and knowing that you're still alive to enjoy another beautiful day on God's planet. This kind of beautiful simplicity is at the heart of this book and these recipes.

The simple and quick recipes in this book are some of my very favorites. When I'm shooting my show or traveling, these are the recipes I turn to. To start out, pick one or two recipes that sound good to you, and try them a few times. In about 30 minutes, you'll have a great meal you can proudly share with your family and friends.

Spend your extra time with your family and friends. Between jobs and responsibilities, we don't make enough time for the people who are most important to us. And we don't make enough time to sit down for dinner with the whole family.

As you spend a little more time with family and friends, you will find out some things of great importance. You'll discover the enjoyment of your little ones (or your younger nieces and nephews) because you're taking the time to listen to one of their very long and great little stories. Believe me, little ones are little for only a short time. Don't miss these irreplaceable times.

Good times and good food. Keeping it simple and keeping it smooth—that's what *Make It Super Simple* is all about. And don't forget the most important thing—take time to kiss the cook.

— G. GARVIN

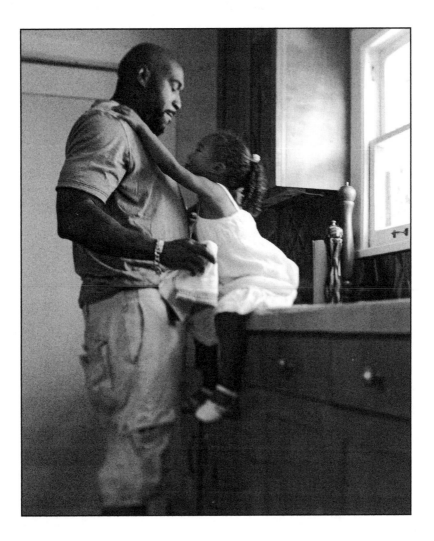

"AND DON'T FORGET THE MOST IMPORTANT THING—
TAKE TIME TO KISS THE COOK."

G's TOP 10
SUPER SIMPLE COOKING SECRETS

1 SHOP FOR SHORTCUTS

Spend a little time roaming the supermarket for items such as packaged salad greens, rice pilaf mixes, precut fruits and veggies, and prepared salsas and sauces. You'll be minutes ahead later.

2 GET A GAME PLAN

You'll get the most done in the least amount of time if you plan ahead. Take a minute to read the recipe and gather everything you need. And always simplify whenever you can. If a recipe calls for chopped or diced garlic, try smashing it instead with the side of a knife blade. While the entrée cooks, toss a salad or set the table.

3 MIX & MATCH

You don't have to make everything from scratch. Go to the store and buy a deli salad to serve with a meat or chicken entrée. Using the right balance of homemade and store-bought adds variety to your meals while keeping everything simple.

4 CHOP, CHOP

When you're chopping onions, carrots, bell peppers, or fresh herbs, chop a little extra to stash in the freezer for busy days.

5 SAUTÉ THE SMART WAY

Sautéing can be a fast, healthy way to cook meat or veggies. The secret of a great sauté is to use a good size skillet or sauté pan and fairly high heat. Cut the food in uniform-size pieces and you'll get the most even cooking.

6 FREEZE WITH EASE

Homemade sauces, such as my stewed plum tomatoes and kalamata sauce on page 54 can easily be doubled. Freeze the sauce in a freezer-safe container to reheat and serve later over your favorite meat or pasta.

7 USE THAT MICROWAVE

It's an easy, no-mess way to melt butter or chocolate, thaw meats and poultry, steam fresh or frozen veggies, or reheat precooked rice or pasta.

8 GET THE KIDS TO HELP

Depending on their ages, they can measure ingredients, whisk and stir dry ingredients and batters, tear herbs, grate cheese, and spread breads. They'll even love to crack eggs for my Bacon-and-Egg Sandwiches on page 78.

9 SPICE IT UP

Seasoning blends are wonderful because you can use them to heighten the flavor of almost any dish with just one measure. I have several of my own blends on the market, including G's Salt Seasoning, Garlic Salt, Lemon Pepper Seasoning, Blackening Spice, BBQ Spice, and Poultry Seasoning. You can order them at www.chefgarvin.com.

10 BE THE CHEF

Most of the dishes in this book leave plenty of room for innovation, so go ahead and experiment with your favorite ingredients or whatever you have on hand. When family and friends come to the table, they'll love it!

NO ALL-NIGHTERS

Hungry for dinner? Throw together one of my super simple, super flavorful meals. Everyone will love you. – G

You just don't have enough time in your day to do everything. Sure, you can write down notes, input reminders to your pda of choice, or tell yourself about all the things you gotta do today (that's me). But the next thing you know, you're asking yourself the million-dollar question: Where did the day go? The answer, my friend, is simple and universally the same: We just don't know. So right from the start of this book, I'm going to help you save time in your day by sharing some of my easiest recipes. I promise you won't spend all night in the kitchen—these meals come together quickly. And please do me a favor: If you figure out where the day went, let me know.

SO MAKE THE MOST OF YOUR TIME IN THE KITCHEN AND GET READY TO ENJOY A DELICIOUS MEAL.

DEEP-DISH BEEF PIE

prep: 30 minutes / bake: 10 minutes / stand: 5 minutes / serves 8

2	prepared 9-inch piecrusts
8	ounces ground beef
8	ounces ground uncooked turkey
1	tablespoon chili powder
1½	teaspoons G's Salt Seasoning
1	teaspoon cumin
1	medium white onion, chopped
½	cup chopped green bell pepper
1½	teaspoons chopped garlic
1	cup canned diced tomatoes, undrained
1½	cups shredded cheddar cheese
1	bunch scallions, chopped
1	egg
1	teaspoon water

1. Preheat oven to 450°F. Bring piecrusts to room temperature. Ease one of the crusts into a 9-inch pie pan. With a fork prick the bottom of the crust in the pan. Bake until crust starts to turn golden. Remove from oven; set aside. Reduce heat to 375°F.

2. Meanwhile, in a medium bowl combine ground beef, ground turkey, chili powder, Salt Seasoning, and cumin. In a medium to large nonstick sauté pan cook ground beef mixture, onion, bell pepper, and garlic until meat is brown and vegetables are tender. Drain off fat. Stir in undrained tomatoes. Fold in cheddar cheese.

3. Place mixture in baked piecrust. Sprinkle with scallions. Cut the bottom out of the other piecrust; place on top of meat mixture. For egg wash, in a small bowl beat together egg and the water. Brush egg wash over piecrust. Bake for 10 to 12 minutes or until crust is golden and filling is bubbly. Remove to wire rack; let stand for 5 to 7 minutes to cool slightly before serving.

CHEESY BAKED BEEF ZITI

prep: 20 minutes / bake: 20 minutes / serves 8

1	16-ounce package dried ziti pasta
1	pound ground beef
	Salt
	Black pepper
	G's Salt Seasoning
1	15-ounce container ricotta cheese
½	cup shredded Parmesan cheese
½	cup shredded cheddar cheese
1	egg, lightly beaten
1	26-ounce jar tomato-base pasta sauce (any flavor)
2	cups shredded mozzarella cheese

1. In a large pot bring water to a boil. Add ziti; cook according to package directions. Drain; return to hot pot. Keep warm.

2. Preheat oven to 350°F. Season ground beef with salt, pepper, and Salt Seasoning. In a large sauté pan cook and stir ground beef until brown; drain off fat. Stir in ricotta cheese, Parmesan cheese, cheddar cheese, and egg. Mix in half of the pasta sauce. Add ziti; toss to mix. Place in a 13×9×2-inch baking pan.

3. Spread the remaining pasta sauce on top of mixture; sprinkle with mozzarella cheese. Bake for 20 to 30 minutes. Cheese should be bubbling and oozing off the sides!

PORK TENDERLOIN IN A TOMATO CREAM SAUCE

prep: 15 minutes / cook: 30 minutes / serves 6

1 pound pork tenderloin, cut into
   1-inch pieces
Kosher salt
Black pepper
Pinch cayenne pepper
1 tablespoon olive oil
3 tablespoons chopped shallots
2 cloves garlic, minced
2 medium green bell peppers,
   seeded and chopped
1 14½-ounce can diced tomatoes,
   undrained
1 8-ounce can tomato sauce
2 tablespoons sugar
2 teaspoons chili powder
1 cup heavy cream
Hot cooked rice

1. Season pork with salt, black pepper, and cayenne pepper. In heavy skillet heat olive oil over medium heat. Add pork, shallots, and garlic to hot oil; sauté until pork is lightly brown. Add bell peppers; sauté for 3 minutes.

2. Meanwhile, break up undrained tomatoes with spoon. Add to mixture in skillet. Stir in tomato sauce, sugar, and chili powder. Bring to a boil; reduce heat. Cover and simmer for 20 minutes, stirring frequently. Uncover and stir in cream. Heat through (do not boil). Serve over hot cooked rice.

RIGATONI WITH SPICY SAUSAGE AND CHICKEN

prep: 15 minutes / cook: 35 minutes / serves 6

Kosher salt

Black pepper

Dash olive oil

1 16-ounce package dried rigatoni pasta

2 tablespoons olive oil

1 pound hot Italian sausage

1 pound boneless, skinless chicken breasts, diced

¼ cup diced green or yellow bell pepper

2 tablespoons chopped garlic

2 tablespoons chopped shallots

2 28-ounce cans plum tomatoes, undrained

½ cup chicken stock

1 15-ounce container ricotta cheese

1 cup shredded mozzarella cheese

1 tablespoon chopped fresh parsley

1. In a large pot bring water to a boil; add pinch salt, pinch black pepper, and the dash olive oil. Add rigatoni; cook according to package directions. Drain; return to hot pot. Keep warm.

2. Meanwhile, for sauce, in another pot heat the 2 tablespoons olive oil over medium heat. Add sausage and chicken; sear on all sides. Add bell pepper, garlic, and shallots; mix well.

3. Add undrained plum tomatoes and chicken stock. Sauté until tomatoes break down. Stir in the ricotta cheese until the mixture becomes creamy. Add rigatoni, tossing to coat with sauce. Stir in mozzarella cheese. Season to taste with additional salt and black pepper. Spoon onto a large platter. Sprinkle with parsley.

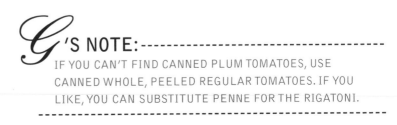

G'S NOTE: ------------------------------------

IF YOU CAN'T FIND CANNED PLUM TOMATOES, USE
CANNED WHOLE, PEELED REGULAR TOMATOES. IF YOU
LIKE, YOU CAN SUBSTITUTE PENNE FOR THE RIGATONI.

TRUFFLE-INFUSED MAC AND CHEESE WITH PROSCIUTTO

prep: 25 minutes / bake: 15 minutes / serves 8

Kosher salt

Black pepper

1 16-ounce package dried
elbow macaroni

3 tablespoons unsalted butter

2 tablespoons minced garlic

2 tablespoons chopped shallots

2 cups milk

2 cups heavy cream

¾ cup shredded sharp
white cheddar cheese

¾ cup grated Parmesan cheese

2 teaspoons truffle oil

8 ounces prosciutto,
cooked until crisp and
coarsely chopped

Hot cooked broccoli or your
favorite vegetable

1. Preheat oven to 350°F. In a large stockpot bring water to a boil; add pinch salt and pinch pepper. Add macaroni; cook according to package directions, slightly undercooking pasta. Drain pasta; rinse with cold water to stop cooking. Drain again; set aside.

2. For cheese sauce, in a medium saucepan heat butter over medium heat until melted. Add garlic and shallots. Sauté until shallots are soft. Add milk and heavy cream. Bring to a boil, stirring constantly. Reduce heat; simmer until the mixture thickens. Whisk in white cheddar cheese and Parmesan cheese. Season mixture with additional salt and pepper. Stir in 1 teaspoon of the truffle oil.

3. Stir cheese sauce into pasta; place pasta mixture in a 13×9×2-inch baking dish. Bake for 10 minutes. Sprinkle crisp-cooked prosciutto over top. Bake 5 to 10 minutes more or until topping is golden brown. Drizzle with the remaining 1 teaspoon truffle oil. Serve with broccoli or your favorite vegetable.

G'S GOTTA-BE-QUICK TIPS:---------------
LOOK FOR PROSCIUTTO AT YOUR SUPERMARKET'S DELI COUNTER OR AN ITALIAN FOOD MARKET. FIND TRUFFLE OIL IN SPECIALTY FOOD SHOPS.

PAN-SEARED BLACKENED PORK CHOPS
start to finish: 30 minutes / serves 4

8   ounces fresh yellow beans
8   ounces fresh green beans
2   tablespoons garlic powder
2   tablespoons onion powder
2   tablespoons G's Blackening
    Spice
    Kosher salt
4   4-ounce boneless pork loin chops
    or rib chops, cut ¾ to 1 inch thick
2   tablespoons olive oil
2   tablespoons unsalted butter
2   tablespoons chopped garlic
2   tablespoons chopped shallots
    Black pepper

1. In a large pot bring water to a boil; add yellow beans and green beans. Cover; cook for 8 to 10 minutes or until beans are nearly crisp-tender. Drain. Place in a bowl of ice water to stop cooking. Drain again. Set aside.

2. In a small bowl combine garlic powder, onion powder, and Blackening Spice. Add salt to taste. Coat both sides of chops with seasoning mixture. In a large skillet heat olive oil over medium-high heat. Reduce heat to medium; add chops. Cook 8 to 12 minutes or until done (160°F), turning once. Remove chops from skillet to a plate. Cover with foil; set aside.

3. Drain skillet. In skillet heat butter over medium heat until melted. Add garlic and shallots; sauté for 1 to 2 minutes or until shallots are soft. Add yellow beans and green beans. Sauté for 4 to 5 minutes more or until beans are crisp-tender. Season with salt and pepper. Serve with chops.

GRILLED CHICKEN WITH PROSCIUTTO
prep: 25 minutes / bake: 5 minutes / serves 4

2   medium red bell peppers,
    seeded and cut into quarters
½   cup olive oil
4   6-ounce boneless, skinless
    chicken breast halves
    Kosher salt
    Cracked black pepper
8   slices prosciutto
2   ounces Roquefort cheese,
    crumbled

1. Preheat oven to 325°F. In a medium bowl toss bell pepper pieces with 2 tablespoons of the olive oil; set aside.

2. In a grill pan heat the remaining 6 tablespoons olive oil. Season the chicken on both sides with the salt and black pepper. Place chicken in hot oil. Cook about 8 minutes or until done (170°F), turning once. Remove chicken from grill pan; set aside.

3. Season bell pepper pieces with salt and black pepper. Place in grill pan; cook until pepper pieces are tender. Arrange chicken on top of pepper pieces. Fold prosciutto slices in half and place two slices on top of each chicken piece. Divide the Roquefort cheese among the chicken pieces. Bake about 5 minutes or until cheese is melted and chicken is heated through.

SWEET AND SOUR CHICKEN OVER WHITE RICE

start to finish: 40 minutes / serves 6

2 cups chicken stock
1 cup uncooked white rice
½ cup water
1½ pounds boneless, skinless chicken breasts or thighs, cut into ½-inch cubes
½ teaspoon kosher salt
½ teaspoon coarse ground black pepper
½ cup all-purpose flour
1 cup canola oil
1 8-ounce can pineapple chunks (juice pack), undrained
¼ cup rice wine vinegar
¼ cup ketchup
1 tablespoon packed light brown sugar
1 tablespoon coconut milk
1 small green bell pepper, seeded and diced
1 small red bell pepper, seeded and diced
1 small white onion, diced

1. In a small saucepan combine 1½ cups of the chicken stock, the rice, and the water. Bring to a boil; reduce heat. Cover and cook for 20 to 25 minutes or until rice has absorbed all of the liquid. Set aside.

2. Meanwhile line a plate with paper towels; set aside. In a bowl combine chicken, salt, and black pepper, tossing to coat. Add flour to chicken; coat well. In a large skillet with deep sides heat canola oil over medium-high heat. Add chicken to hot oil; cook until brown. Using a slotted spoon, transfer chicken to paper towel-lined plate; set aside.

3. In a medium saucepan combine undrained pineapple chunks, the remaining ½ cup chicken stock, the rice wine vinegar, ketchup, brown sugar, and coconut milk. Bring to a boil; reduce heat. Stir to combine; simmer for 3 minutes. Add bell peppers and onion. Cook for 5 minutes more. Stir in chicken; cook for 5 to 10 minutes more or until chicken is done. Serve over hot cooked rice.

CITRUS-MARINATED CHICKEN OVER MESCLUN

prep: 10 minutes / marinate: 10 minutes / cook: 15 minutes / serves 4

3   tablespoons olive oil
    Balsamic vinegar
1   tablespoon chopped
      fresh tarragon
1   tablespoon red wine vinegar
1   tablespoon cider vinegar
1   tablespoon orange juice
1   tablespoon honey
1   teaspoon lime juice
1   teaspoon lemon juice
4   6-ounce boneless, skinless
      chicken breast halves
2   teaspoons G's Salt Seasoning
    Canola oil cooking spray
1   pint cherry tomatoes, halved
1   5- to 8-ounce bag mesclun greens
1   6-ounce can mandarin
      oranges, drained

1. For marinade, in a large bowl whisk together 2 tablespoons of the olive oil, 2 tablespoons balsamic vinegar, the tarragon, red wine vinegar, cider vinegar, orange juice, honey, lime juice, and lemon juice.

2. Sprinkle chicken with Salt Seasoning. Add chicken to marinade; let stand for 10 minutes. Remove chicken from marinade. Discard marinade.

3. Coat a nonstick grill pan with cooking spray; heat pan over medium-high heat. Place chicken in grill pan; cook about 15 minutes or until done (170°F), turning once.

4. Meanwhile, drizzle cherry tomatoes with the remaining 1 tablespoon olive oil and additional balsamic vinegar to taste, tossing to coat. Arrange greens on four dinner plates. Divide cherry tomatoes among the plates. Add a chicken breast half and mandarin oranges to each plate.

SEE PHOTO, PAGE 34

G'S NOTE: -------------------------------------
IF YOU LIKE, USE 1 TEASPOON DRIED TARRAGON IN
PLACE OF THE FRESH TARRAGON.

HERB-CRUSTED PARMESAN CHICKEN BREASTS

prep: 20 minutes / bake: 20 minutes / serves 6

6   boneless, skinless chicken
      breast halves
2   tablespoons unsalted butter
2   tablespoons olive oil
1½   cups dry bread crumbs
6   tablespoons chopped fresh basil
3   tablespoons chopped
      fresh parsley
4½   teaspoons chopped
      fresh rosemary
1   tablespoon chopped fresh thyme
1   tablespoon garlic powder
1½   teaspoons kosher salt
½   teaspoon black pepper
½   cup shaved Parmesan cheese

1. Preheat oven to 450°F. Place each chicken breast half between two sheets of plastic wrap. Using the flat side of a meat mallet, pound chicken to a ½- to ¾-inch thickness (see photo below). In a small saucepan heat butter and olive oil over medium heat until butter is melted; cool slightly.

2. In a shallow bowl mix bread crumbs, basil, parsley, rosemary, thyme, garlic powder, salt, and pepper. Brush chicken pieces on both sides with melted butter mixture. Coat chicken pieces on both sides with bread crumb mixture. Place chicken pieces on a baking sheet.

3. Bake chicken for 15 to 20 minutes or until done (170°F) and bread crumbs are golden. Top with shaved Parmesan cheese; bake about 5 minutes more or until cheese is golden.

G'S GOTTA-BE-QUICK TIP:------------------

THE SLICKEST WAY TO SHAVE PARMESAN CHEESE IS TO USE A VEGETABLE PEELER.

HONEY-MUSTARD CHICKEN

prep: 20 minutes / bake: 30 minutes / cool: 10 minutes / serves 4

4	boneless, skinless chicken breast halves
2	tablespoons garlic powder
	Kosher salt
	Black pepper
½	cup honey
½	cup Dijon mustard
¼	cup apple juice
2	shallots, diced
1	teaspoon paprika
¼	teaspoon chopped fresh parsley
3	tablespoons olive oil
1	large zucchini, sliced into ½-inch pieces
1	large red bell pepper, seeded and sliced into ½-inch strips
1	pound fresh asparagus, cut into 2-inch pieces

1. Preheat oven to 350°F. Lightly grease a 13×9×2-inch baking dish. Sprinkle chicken with 1 tablespoon of the garlic powder. Season with salt and black pepper. Place chicken in prepared baking dish.

2. In small bowl combine honey, Dijon mustard, apple juice, shallots, paprika, and parsley. Brush half of the mixture over chicken. Bake for 15 minutes. Turn chicken pieces over; brush with the remaining honey-mustard mixture. Bake for 15 minutes more or until done (170°F). Cool for 10 minutes before serving.

3. Meanwhile lightly coat a grill pan with some of the olive oil; heat over medium heat. In large bowl combine zucchini, bell pepper, and asparagus. Toss with the remaining 1 tablespoon garlic powder and the remaining olive oil. Season with salt and black pepper. Mix, making sure all vegetables are evenly coated. Place vegetables in the grill pan. Sauté for 4 to 6 minutes or until vegetables are tender. Serve along with chicken.

G'S QUICK CHICKEN STIR-FRY

prep: 25 minutes / stand: 15 minutes / cook: 10 minutes / serves 4

12   ounces boneless, skinless
     chicken breasts, cut into
     thin strips
¼   cup soy sauce
2   tablespoons cornstarch
2   cloves garlic, chopped
½   teaspoon minced fresh ginger
¾   cup water
¼   cup vegetable oil
1   medium red bell pepper, seeded
     and sliced into bite-size strips
1   medium green bell pepper,
     seeded and sliced into
     bite-size strips
1   medium yellow bell pepper,
     seeded and sliced into
     bite-size strips
1   medium onion, sliced
4   ounces fresh mushrooms, sliced
4   ounces fresh sugar snap peas
     Hot cooked rice

1. In a medium bowl combine chicken, 2 tablespoons of the soy sauce, the cornstarch, garlic, and ginger; let stand for 15 minutes. Meanwhile, in a small bowl combine the remaining 2 tablespoons soy sauce and the water.

2. In a wok or large sauté pan heat 2 tablespoons of the vegetable oil over medium-high heat. Add chicken and stir-fry about 3 minutes or until done. Remove chicken from wok. Heat the remaining 2 tablespoons vegetable oil in same pan. Add bell peppers, onion, mushrooms, and sugar snap peas; stir-fry for 5 minutes.

3. Stir chicken and soy sauce mixture into wok. Bring mixture to a boil; stirring constantly. Boil for 1 minute. Serve over hot cooked rice.

PARMESAN BOW-TIE PASTA

prep: 20 minutes / cook: 17 minutes / serves 6

2   tablespoons olive oil
    Pinch salt
    Pinch black pepper
1   12-ounce package dried
      bow-tie pasta
2   tablespoons unsalted butter
3   tablespoons chopped garlic
2   tablespoons chopped shallots
3   cups sliced fresh mushrooms
¼   cup diced red bell pepper
1   cup diced pancetta
1   cup light cream
1   cup frozen peas, thawed
1   cup shredded Parmesan cheese

1. In a large pot bring water to a boil; add olive oil, salt, and black pepper. Add pasta; cook according to package directions. Drain; return to hot pot. Keep warm.

2. Meanwhile, for cream sauce, in a large skillet heat butter over medium heat until melted. Stir in garlic and shallots. Add mushrooms and bell pepper. Sauté for 2 to 3 minutes or until vegetables get soft. Remove vegetable mixture from skillet; set aside.

3. In the same skillet cook pancetta until crispy; drain off fat. Return vegetable mixture to skillet, mixing all ingredients well. Slowly add cream. Simmer for 5 minutes. Stir in peas. Slowly stir in ½ cup of the Parmesan cheese. Simmer until heated through. Place pasta in a large serving bowl; pour cream sauce over pasta. Sprinkle with the remaining ½ cup Parmesan cheese.

CHICKEN-AND-BROCCOLI CASSEROLE

prep: 35 minutes / bake: 25 minutes / serves 8

1   16-ounce package dried medium
      egg noodles
1   14-ounce package frozen broccoli
      florets, thawed
2   tablespoons unsalted butter
2   tablespoons all-purpose flour
1   teaspoon yellow mustard
    Salt
    Black pepper
2   cups milk
1   cup shredded sharp
      cheddar cheese
3   cups chopped cooked chicken
½   cup shredded mozzarella cheese
    Paprika

1. In a large pot bring water to a boil. Add noodles; cook according to package directions. Drain; return to hot pot. Keep warm. In a large saucepan cook broccoli according to package directions; drain. Keep warm.

2. Preheat oven to 350°F. For cheese sauce, in a medium saucepan melt butter; blend in flour and yellow mustard. Season with salt and pepper. Stir in milk. Cook, stirring constantly, until thickened. Remove from heat; whisk in cheddar cheese until melted.

3. In a 3-quart casserole layer cooked noodles, broccoli, and chicken. Pour cheese sauce over all. Sprinkle mozzarella cheese on top. Sprinkle with paprika. Bake about 25 minutes or until bubbling hot.

CHICKEN STEW WITH POTATOES AND VEGETABLES

prep: 25 minutes / cook: 40 minutes / serves 8

2 tablespoons olive oil
1 4- to 5-pound roasting chicken,
  cut up
1 cup chicken stock
½ cup dry sherry
2 teaspoons salt
½ teaspoon black pepper
10 pearl onions, halved
1 large red bell pepper, seeded
  and diced
1 cup frozen peas
1 cup sliced carrots
1 cup diced potatoes
½ cup diced fresh asparagus
½ cup fresh or frozen corn
2 tablespoons smashed garlic
½ cup cold water
3 tablespoons cornstarch
  Hot cooked rice
1 tablespoon chopped fresh parsley

1. In a stockpot heat olive oil. Add the chicken; brown on all sides.
2. Add chicken stock, sherry, salt, and black pepper to stockpot. Bring to boiling; reduce heat. Cover and simmer for 30 minutes. Add onions, bell pepper, peas, carrots, potatoes, asparagus, corn, and garlic. Return to boiling; reduce heat to simmer.
3. Meanwhile, in a small bowl combine the cold water and cornstarch. Stir into mixture in stockpot. Continue cooking about 10 minutes or until vegetables are tender and stew is thickened. Serve over hot cooked rice. Sprinkle with parsley.

OVEN-ROASTED CHICKEN WITH MUSHROOM RAGOÛT

prep: 30 minutes / bake: 10 minutes / serves 4

8   boneless, skinless chicken thighs
    Kosher salt
    Cracked black pepper
½   cup olive oil
12 cloves garlic, smashed
    Mushroom Ragoût

1. Preheat oven to 350°F. Season both sides of chicken thighs with salt and pepper. In an oven-going skillet heat olive oil over medium heat. Add smashed garlic; top with chicken. Sear chicken on one side for 5 minutes; turn chicken over. Bake for 10 to 15 minutes or until done (180°F).

2. Serve Mushroom Ragoût over chicken.

MUSHROOM RAGOÛT: In a medium sauté pan heat ¼ cup olive oil over medium heat. Add 1 cup fresh button mushrooms, coarsely chopped; 1 cup fresh shiitake mushrooms, coarsely chopped; 1 cup fresh morel mushrooms, coarsely chopped; 1 tablespoon minced garlic; and 1 tablespoon diced shallots. Sauté for 5 minutes. Add 1 cup white wine; simmer for 2 minutes. Add ½ cup (1 stick) unsalted butter and 2 tablespoons chopped fresh thyme. Season to taste with salt and pepper.

𝒢'S NOTE: --

IF MOREL MUSHROOMS ARE OUT OF SEASON,
SUBSTITUTE CREMINI OR OTHER WILD MUSHROOMS.

SAUTÉED LEMON CHICKEN WITH HERBS

prep: 15 minutes / cook: 9 minutes / serves 4

4   6-ounce boneless, skinless
      chicken breast halves
      Kosher salt
      Cracked white pepper
2   tablespoons chopped fresh
      rosemary
2   tablespoons chopped fresh thyme
2   tablespoons chopped fresh
      flat-leaf parsley
½   cup olive oil
1   cup white wine
1½   cups lemon juice
3   tablespoons unsalted butter

1. Season chicken on both sides with salt and pepper. On a dry flat plate combine rosemary, thyme, and parsley. Dip top sides of chicken into herb mixture, being sure to pat the herb mixture so it sticks to chicken.

2. In a medium sauté pan heat olive oil over medium heat. Place the chicken in hot oil, herb sides down. Sauté for 1 minute. Turn chicken; cook for 3 minutes more. Add wine; simmer for 2 minutes. Turn heat to a low simmer. Add lemon juice and butter; cook about 3 minutes or until chicken is done (160°F).

ROASTED BBQ CHICKEN WITH FRENCH FRIES

prep: 30 minutes / bake: 30 minutes / cook: 5 minutes per batch fries / serves 6

4   Kennebec potatoes or other
      all-purpose potatoes, peeled
      and sliced lengthwise
6   6-ounce chicken thighs with skin
      G's BBQ Spice Rub
6   to 8 cups peanut oil
6   cloves garlic, smashed
2   cups bourbon-flavored barbecue
      sauce
      Salt

1. Preheat oven to 350°F. Place potatoes in a bowl of cold water; set aside. Season chicken with BBQ Spice Rub.

2. In an oven-going skillet heat ½ cup of the peanut oil over medium heat. Add chicken, skin sides down, and garlic; sear for 6 to 8 minutes; turn chicken over. Bake for 20 minutes. Pour barbecue sauce over the chicken; bake about 10 minutes more or until chicken is done (180°F).

3. Meanwhile drain potatoes well. In medium saucepan heat remaining 5½ to 7½ cups peanut oil to 365°F. Cook one-fourth of the potatoes in the hot oil until crispy and golden. Using a slotted spoon, remove potatoes from oil. Drain on paper towels. Season with salt. Repeat with remaining potatoes. Serve with chicken.

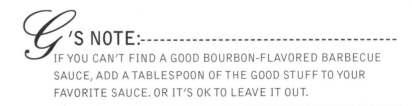

G'S NOTE:

IF YOU CAN'T FIND A GOOD BOURBON-FLAVORED BARBECUE SAUCE, ADD A TABLESPOON OF THE GOOD STUFF TO YOUR FAVORITE SAUCE. OR IT'S OK TO LEAVE IT OUT.

CITRUS-MARINATED CHICKEN
OVER MESCLUN
RECIPE ON PAGE 25

GRILLED SWORDFISH WITH STEWED
PLUM TOMATOES AND KALAMATA OLIVES
RECIPE ON PAGE 54

BEET SALAD (ABOVE)
RECIPE ON PAGE 99
PEPPERED SHRIMP WRAPS (RIGHT)
RECIPE ON PAGE 91
BRIOCHE FRIES (RIGHT)
RECIPE ON PAGE 111

Blackening Spice

GRILLED T-BONE STEAKS WITH
PARSLEY-AND-GARLIC SAUCE (LEFT)
RECIPE ON PAGE 132 AND
ROASTED POTATOES (LEFT)
RECIPE ON PAGE 105
G. GARVIN SPICES FOR SALE AT WWW.CHEFGARVIN.COM

BLACK BEAN, TORTILLA, AND CHEDDAR SOUP (ABOVE)
RECIPE ON PAGE 76
WARM CHEDDAR CHEESE GRITS WITH SHRIMP, PANCETTA, AND SCALLIONS (RIGHT)
RECIPE ON PAGE 207

TOMATOES-AND-MOZZARELLA SALAD
WITH BALSAMIC VINAIGRETTE
RECIPE ON PAGE 78

BBQ SPICE-RUBBED PORK LOIN AND ZESTY SALSA
RECIPE ON PAGE 137 AND
STRING BEANS WITH GARLIC AND ALMONDS
RECIPE ON PAGE 100

BLACKENED PORK CHOPS WITH
STEWED CHERRY TOMATOES AND BASIL
RECIPE ON PAGE 84

PAN-ROASTED CHICKEN WITH TOMATO RAGOÛT

prep: 15 minutes / cook: 20 minutes / serves 6

6   6-ounce boneless, skinless
      chicken thighs
    Kosher salt
    Cracked black pepper
½   cup olive oil
1   medium sweet onion (such as
      Vidalia, Maui, or Walla Walla),
      coarsely chopped
5   cloves garlic, smashed
2   red heirloom tomatoes,
      coarsely chopped
1   yellow heirloom tomato,
      coarsely chopped
1   green heirloom tomato,
      coarsely chopped
2   cups water

1. Season chicken on both sides with salt and pepper. In a large sauté pan heat ¼ cup of the olive oil over medium heat. Add chicken to hot oil; sauté for 8 minutes, turning once.
2. Add the remaining ¼ cup olive oil; add onion and garlic. Stir in tomatoes; sauté for 4 minutes. Season with salt and pepper.
3. Add the water; bring to a boil. Reduce heat; simmer until tomatoes are soft and chicken is done (180°F).

G'S NOTE: ------------------------------
VISIT YOUR LOCAL FARMER'S MARKET OR GOURMET
FOOD MARKET TO FIND HEIRLOOM TOMATOES. ONLY BUY
TOMATOES THAT YOU WILL CONSUME IN A FEW DAYS SINCE
THEY LOSE THEIR FLAVOR WHEN STORED IN THE FRIDGE.
KEEP THEM OUT OF DIRECT SUNLIGHT ON THE COUNTER.

MARINATED TURKEY CUTLETS
WITH ROASTED POTATOES AND STEAMED BROCCOLI

prep: 20 minutes / marinate: 10 minutes / cook: 16 minutes / bake: 45 minutes / serves 4

2 tablespoons cider vinegar

½ teaspoon G's Lemon
   Pepper Seasoning

½ teaspoon dried thyme

½ teaspoon granulated garlic

½ teaspoon dried sage

 G's Salt Seasoning

1 pound turkey breast tenderloin

 Salt

½ of a head fresh broccoli,
   cut into spears

 Black pepper

2 tablespoons olive oil

 Roasted Potatoes

1. In a small bowl combine cider vinegar, Lemon Pepper Seasoning, thyme, granulated garlic, and sage. Season with Salt Seasoning. Cut turkey breast tenderloin in half horizontally. Place turkey in a resealable plastic bag; pour vinegar mixture over turkey. Seal bag. Let stand for 10 minutes, turning occasionally.

2. In a medium pot bring a small amount of water to a boil; add salt. Add broccoli; cook for 8 to 10 minutes or until broccoli is tender. Drain broccoli; season with salt and pepper to taste. Set aside.

3. Remove turkey from vinegar mixture. In a large skillet heat oil over medium heat; add turkey. Cook for 8 to 10 minutes or until done (170°F), turning once.

4. Serve turkey with Roasted Potatoes and cooked broccoli.

ROASTED POTATOES: Heat oven to 325°F. In a bowl toss 1 pound Yukon gold potatoes, quartered, with 1½ teaspoons olive oil and ½ teaspoon Salt Seasoning. Transfer to a shallow baking pan. Bake about 45 minutes or until potatoes are tender and brown on the edges, stirring once halfway through baking time.

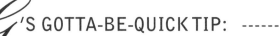

G'S GOTTA-BE-QUICK TIP: ----------------
FOR A SUPER SIMPLE SHORTCUT, USE A 20-OUNCE PACKAGE FROZEN ROASTED RUSSET POTATO PIECES IN PLACE OF THE YUKON GOLD POTATOES AND A 9- TO 10-OUNCE PACKAGE FROZEN BROCCOLI SPEARS COOKED ACCORDING TO PACKAGE DIRECTIONS INSTEAD OF THE FRESH BROCCOLI.

RIGATONI WITH TURKEY SAUSAGE AND VEGETABLES

prep: 20 minutes / cook: 15 minutes / serves 6

1   16-ounce package dried
    rigatoni pasta
1   pound Italian turkey sausage
    links, cut into ½-inch slices
1   small onion, cut into thin wedges
1   clove garlic, minced
1   9-ounce package frozen sugar
    snap peas, thawed
1   medium yellow bell pepper,
    seeded and cut into 1-inch
    pieces
1   medium green bell pepper,
    seeded and cut into 1-inch
    pieces
½   cup chicken stock
    Chopped fresh basil
    Salt
    Black pepper
4   plum tomatoes, chopped
2   tablespoons olive oil
    Shredded mozzarella cheese

1. In a pot bring water to a boil. Add rigatoni; cook according to package directions. Drain; return to hot pot. Keep warm.

2. Meanwhile, in a large skillet cook sausage over medium-high heat for 5 minutes, stirring occasionally. Drain off fat. Stir onion and garlic into sausage; cook and stir for 3 minutes. Add sugar snap peas, bell peppers, and chicken stock. Season with basil; mix well.

3. Bring to a boil; reduce heat. Simmer for 3 or 5 minutes or until sausage is done. Season with salt and black pepper. Add tomatoes and olive oil. Cook over medium-low heat for 3 to 5 minutes or until bubbly, stirring occasionally. Toss with rigatoni. Transfer to a serving bowl. Sprinkle with mozzarella.

SAUTÉED STRIPED BASS WITH CABBAGE AND SCALLIONS

prep: 15 minutes / cook: 8 minutes / serves 6

6	6-ounce pieces fresh striped bass, skin scored
	Kosher salt
	Cracked white pepper
½	cup olive oil
¼	cup (½ stick) unsalted butter
2	teaspoons minced garlic
2	teaspoons diced shallots
6	to 8 cups shredded napa cabbage
6	scallions, bias-cut into small pieces

1. Rinse fish; pat dry with paper towels. Season fish on both sides with salt and pepper. In a large sauté pan heat 6 tablespoons of the olive oil over medium heat. Place fish pieces, skin sides down, in hot oil. Sear for 4 minutes; turn fish over. Reduce heat to medium-low; sauté for 1 minute. Reduce heat to very low. Sauté for 3 to 5 minutes more or until done, turning fish as needed to brown evenly.

2. Meanwhile in another sauté pan heat the remaining 2 tablespoons olive oil over medium heat. Add butter, garlic, and shallots. Heat until butter melts; stir in cabbage. Quickly sauté for 3 minutes. Stir in scallions.

3. To serve, divide cabbage mixture among six dinner plates. Top each with a piece of fish.

SAUTÉED SALMON WITH BUTTERED TRIO OF BELL PEPPERS

prep: 30 minutes / bake: 5 minutes / serves 4

4	6-ounce fresh salmon fillets with skin
	Kosher salt
	Cracked black pepper
½	cup olive oil
2	teaspoons minced garlic
1	large red bell pepper, seeded and sliced lengthwise
1	large yellow bell pepper, seeded and sliced lengthwise
1	large green bell pepper, seeded and sliced lengthwise
3	tablespoons unsalted butter

1. Preheat oven to 325°F. Rinse fish; pat dry with paper towels. Season fish on all sides with salt and black pepper. In a large sauté pan heat ¼ cup of the olive oil over medium heat. Place fish, skin sides down, in hot oil. Sauté about 5 minutes or until the skin is seared. Turn fish; sauté for 2 minutes. Turn fish back to skin side. Bake about 5 minutes or until done.

2. In another sauté pan heat the remaining ¼ cup olive oil over medium heat; add garlic. Sauté for 1 minute. Add bell peppers; sprinkle with salt and black pepper. Sauté about 5 minutes or until peppers are tender. Add butter; heat until butter is melted.

3. To serve, place pepper mixture on a large platter. Top with fish.

BAKED ALASKAN HALIBUT WITH HERBED VEGETABLES

prep: 15 minutes / bake: 30 minutes / serves 4

1   pound skinless fresh
    halibut fillets
2   medium zucchini, sliced into
    1-inch-thick pieces
1   green bell pepper, seeded and
    sliced
1   cup sliced fresh mushrooms
½   of a medium onion, chopped
3   tablespoons unsalted
    butter, melted
1   tablespoon lemon juice
1   tablespoon chopped fresh basil
¼   teaspoon salt
⅛   teaspoon black pepper
    Hot cooked rice

1. Preheat oven to 350°F. Rinse fish; pat dry with paper towels. Place fish in an 8×8×2-inch baking pan. Place zucchini, bell pepper, mushrooms, and onion around and over fish.

2. In small bowl stir together butter, lemon juice, basil, salt, and black pepper; pour over fish.

3. Bake for 30 to 40 minutes or until done. Serve over hot cooked rice.

G'S NOTE: ---
YOU CAN SUBSTITUTE ANY VEGETABLES YOU LIKE
FOR THE ZUCCHINI, BELL PEPPER, MUSHROOMS, AND
ONION. HOW ABOUT THINLY SLICED CARROTS, PEA PODS,
BROCCOLI FLORETS, AND CUT ASPARAGUS?

GRILLED SWORDFISH WITH STEWED PLUM TOMATOES AND KALAMATA OLIVES

prep: 10 minutes / cook: 23 minutes / serves 4

4   6-ounce skinless fresh
     swordfish fillets
     Kosher salt
     Cracked black pepper
½   cup olive oil
9   plum tomatoes, halved
½   cup chopped fresh basil
6   cloves garlic, smashed
½   cup (1 stick) unsalted butter
½   cup kalamata olives, pitted and
     coarsely chopped

1. Rinse fish; pat dry with paper towels. Season the fish on both sides with the salt and pepper. In a grill pan heat 2 tablespoons of the olive oil over medium-high heat. Add fish to hot oil; cook for 5 minutes; turn fish over and cook about 5 minutes more or until done. Remove from grill pan; set aside.

2. In a medium sauté pan heat ¼ cup of the olive oil over medium heat. Add tomatoes, basil, and garlic to hot oil. Season with salt and pepper. Cover and simmer for 10 minutes. Turn heat to low; whisk in butter. Stir in olives.

3. To serve, spoon tomato mixture on top of fish. Drizzle with the remaining 2 tablespoons olive oil.

SEE PHOTO, PAGE 36-37

G'S NOTE:--------------------------------------
IF YOU CAN'T GET SWORDFISH, HALIBUT IS A GOOD
SUBSTITUTE. THIS ZESTY SAUCE ALSO IS TERRIFIC OVER
CHICKEN OR PASTA.

BLACKENED TROUT WITH TOASTED WALNUTS AND TARTAR SAUCE

prep: 20 minutes / bake: 4 minutes / serves 3

1   cup mayonnaise
2   tablespoons sweet pickle relish
1   tablespoon chopped fresh parsley
1   tablespoon lemon juice
     Pinch G's Garlic Salt
3   8-ounce skinless fresh
        trout fillets
¼   cup G's Blackening Spice
¼   cup olive oil
½   cup walnut halves

1. Preheat oven to 350°F. For tartar sauce, in a medium bowl combine mayonnaise, pickle relish, parsley, lemon juice, and Garlic Salt; set aside.

2. Rinse fish; pat dry with paper towels. Season fish with Blackening Spice on the flesh side only. In a large oven-going skillet heat olive oil over medium-high heat.

3. Place fish fillets, flesh sides down, in hot oil. Sauté for 3 minutes; turn fish over. Bake about 4 minutes more or until done. Sprinkle with walnuts. Serve tartar sauce on top of fish.

BAKED BLACKENED CATFISH

prep: 20 minutes / bake: 15 minutes / serves 3 or 4

6   to 8 catfish fillets, thinly sliced
2   teaspoons cayenne pepper
1   teaspoon salt
1   teaspoon garlic powder
1   teaspoon onion powder
1   teaspoon dried thyme, crushed
1   teaspoon paprika
1   teaspoon lemon pepper
1   teaspoon black pepper
2   tablespoons butter, melted
1   cup bottled Italian salad dressing
     Olive oil

1. Preheat oven to 350°F. Lightly grease a 13×9×2-inch baking dish. Rinse fish; pat dry with paper towels.

2. For seasoning, in a small bowl combine cayenne pepper, salt, garlic powder, onion powder, thyme, paprika, lemon pepper, and black pepper. Brush one side of each fish fillet with melted butter; sprinkle with seasoning. Repeat on the other side, coating each fillet completely.

3. Heat a cast-iron skillet over medium-high heat. Add any remaining butter to skillet. If needed, add up to 2 tablespoons olive oil. Place fish fillets in skillet; sauté about 4 minutes or until blackened, turning once. Transfer fish to baking dish. Drizzle with Italian salad dressing. Bake about 15 minutes or until done.

G'S GOTTA-BE-QUICK TIP:

BE SURE TO BUY THE TROUT IN FILLET FORM (COMPLETELY OFF THE BONE) FROM YOUR FISH GUY. FOR A RICHER NUT FLAVOR, TOAST THE WALNUTS BEFORE YOU START BAKING THE FISH.

STEAMED HALIBUT WITH SPINACH, ARTICHOKE HEARTS, AND PAPRIKA BUTTER

prep: 30 minutes / bake: 17 minutes / serves 8

2 pounds fresh spinach
   Kosher salt
   Cracked black pepper
2 pounds skinless fresh Alaskan halibut, bias-cut into ½-inch-thick portions
2 8- to 9-ounce packages frozen artichoke hearts, thawed
3 tablespoons minced garlic
1 cup (2 sticks) unsalted butter, softened
¼ cup chopped fresh chives
¼ cup chopped fresh rosemary
   Paprika

1. Preheat oven to 375°F. Place spinach in a large oven-going skillet. Season spinach with salt and pepper. Rinse fish; pat dry with paper towels. Shingle the fish pieces on top of the spinach. Season fish with salt and pepper. Place artichoke hearts on top of halibut (see photo below). Sprinkle with 1 tablespoon of the garlic. Bake for 14 minutes.

2. Meanwhile, in a medium bowl combine softened butter, the remaining 2 tablespoons garlic, the chives and rosemary. Season with paprika. Place in the freezer for 5 minutes.

3. Remove skillet from oven. Place some of the butter mixture on each piece of fish. Bake for 3 to 6 minutes more or until fish is done. Serve immediately.

G'S GOTTA-BE-QUICK TIP: -----------------
BE SURE TO USE FROZEN ARTICHOKE HEARTS TO SAVE PREPARATION TIME, AND HAVE THE MARKET PRECUT YOUR FISH.

PAN-SEARED TILAPIA WITH LEMON AND THYME

prep: 10 minutes / cook: 13 minutes / serves 6

6 6-ounce skinless fresh
   tilapia fillets
   Kosher salt
   Ground white pepper
1 cup all-purpose flour
5 to 6 tablespoons olive oil
¼ cup white wine
¾ cup (1½ sticks) unsalted
   butter, cut up
¼ cup lemon juice
1 tablespoon chopped fresh thyme
   Hot cooked rice (optional)

1. Rinse fish; pat dry with paper towels. Season fish with salt and pepper. Dredge fish with flour, shaking off excess.
2. In a large sauté pan heat olive oil over medium heat. Add fish to hot oil; sauté for 6 minutes, turning once. Pour wine into pan; simmer for 4 minutes.
3. Stir in butter and lemon juice. Simmer for 3 to 4 minutes more or until fish is done. Add thyme. If desired, serve fish over hot cooked rice.

G'S GOTTA-BE-QUICK TIP: ------------------
TO ENSURE THE FRESH THYME IS READY WHEN YOU
NEED IT, CHOP IT BEFORE STARTING THE RECIPE.

FETTUCCINE WITH CLAMS,
CRISPY BACON, AND SHALLOTS

start to finish: 25 minutes / serves 4

12	small clams in shells
	Kosher salt
1	16-ounce package dried fettuccine pasta
1	cup diced bacon
3	medium shallots, diced
2	cups white wine
2	tablespoons unsalted butter
	Cracked white pepper

1. Scrub clams under cold running water. Set aside.

2. In a large pot bring water to a boil; add salt. Add fettuccine; cook according to package directions. Drain; return to hot pot. Keep warm.

3. Meanwhile, in a large sauté pan cook bacon about 4 minutes or until crisp; drain bacon on paper towels. Reserve one-fourth of the bacon drippings in pan. Add clams and shallots. Pour in wine. Cover and cook about 7 minutes or until clams open. Add cooked pasta, bacon, and butter; toss until pasta is coated. Season with salt and pepper.

PAN-SEARED SOLE WITH ROSEMARY,
THYME, AND BROWN BUTTER

prep: 10 minutes / cook: 10 minutes / serves 6

4	8-ounce skinless fresh Dover sole fillets
	Kosher salt
	Cracked black pepper
1	cup all-purpose flour
½	cup olive oil
1	cup (2 sticks) unsalted butter
1	tablespoon chopped fresh rosemary
1	tablespoon chopped fresh thyme

1. Rinse fish; pat dry with paper towels. Season fish on both sides with salt and pepper. Dredge in flour, shaking off excess. In a large nonstick sauté pan heat olive oil over medium heat.

2. Place fish in hot oil; sauté for 3 minutes. Reduce heat to medium-low; turn fish over. Cook about 5 minutes more or until done. Transfer fish to a serving platter.

3. Add butter, rosemary, and thyme to sauté pan. Cook over medium heat until butter turns brown (do not burn). Pour butter and herbs over fish.

G'S SERVING NOTE:--------------------------
THIS FISH GOES GREAT WITH STRING BEANS WITH GARLIC AND ALMONDS (SEE RECIPE, PAGE 100).

QUICK FRIED SCALLOPS AND PEA PODS
OVER BUTTERED LINGUINE

start to finish: 25 minutes / serves 4

1	16-ounce package dried linguine pasta
½	cup (1 stick) unsalted butter
1	teaspoon granulated garlic
5	slices bacon, diced
1	pound fresh bay scallops
1	teaspoon G's Salt Seasoning
½	of a 10-ounce bag shredded carrots
1	bunch scallions, cut into ½-inch pieces
1	6-ounce package frozen pea pods, thawed
1	teaspoon chopped fresh ginger
1	tablespoon teriyaki sauce

1. In a large pot bring water to a boil. Add linguine; cook according to package directions. Drain; return to hot pot. Add butter and garlic; toss to coat linguine. Keep warm.

2. Preheat a large wok or nonstick skillet over medium-high heat. Add bacon; cook until crisp. Remove bacon; set aside.

3. Rinse scallops; pat dry with paper towels. Season scallops with Salt Seasoning. Add to skillet; sauté for 2 minutes. Add carrots and scallions. Sauté for 2 to 3 minutes more or until vegetables are hot. Stir in pea pods and ginger. Stir in teriyaki sauce and cooked bacon; heat through. Serve over linguine mixture.

SPICY CRAB-AND-SHRIMP FRITTATA

prep: 15 minutes / cook: 17 minutes / stand: 10 minutes / serves 6

8   eggs
2   tablespoons grated
    Parmesan cheese
1   teaspoon black pepper
½   teaspoon kosher salt
8   ounces fresh medium
    shrimp in their shells
1   tablespoon olive oil
1   tablespoon unsalted butter
8   ounces lump crabmeat
½   cup chopped scallions
1½ cups shredded pepper
    Jack cheese

1. Preheat broiler. In a medium bowl whisk together eggs, Parmesan cheese, pepper, and salt until well blended. Set aside. Clean shrimp, removing shells; use tip of sharp knife to remove veins (see photo below). In a 10-inch broilerproof skillet heat olive oil and butter over medium-high heat until butter is melted. Add shrimp; sauté for 3 to 5 minutes or until shrimp is done and orange in color. Stir in crabmeat and scallions.

2. Pour egg mixture evenly over mixture in skillet. Sprinkle with pepper Jack cheese. Reduce heat to medium-low. As mixture begins to set, run a spatula around the skillet edge, lifting egg mixture so uncooked portion flows underneath. Continue cooking and lifting edge until egg mixture is almost set (surface will be moist).

3. Once eggs are firm and light brown on the bottom (edge will pull away from the side of the skillet), place skillet under broiler. Broil about 2 minutes or until frittata is golden brown. Place skillet on wire rack; let stand for 10 minutes before serving.

G'S NOTE:--
THIS DISH CAN BE SERVED WITH YOUR FAVORITE
BREAD, RICE, VEGETABLE, OR GRAPES AS
ACCOMPANIMENTS.

G'S SUPER SIMPLE GARLIC SHRIMP

prep: 15 minutes / cook: 7 minutes / serves 6

2   pounds fresh small shrimp in
    their shells
    Salt
    Paprika
¼   cup olive oil
4   cloves garlic, minced
    Crushed red pepper
¾   cup white wine
2   teaspoons lemon juice
    Hot cooked rice
    Chopped fresh parsley

1. Clean shrimp, removing shells; use tip of sharp knife to remove veins (see photo at left). Season with salt and paprika.

2. In a large sauté pan heat olive oil over medium heat. Add garlic and crushed red pepper to hot oil. Sauté just until garlic is beginning to brown. Add shrimp. Cook, stirring constantly, for 3 to 5 minutes or until shrimp is done and orange in color.

3. Reduce heat to low. Stir in wine and lemon juice. Simmer for 3 to 5 minutes or until desired consistency. Serve immediately over hot cooked rice. Sprinkle with parsley.

JUMBO SHRIMP WITH FETA CHEESE AND TOMATO SAUCE

prep: 25 minutes / bake: 7 minutes / serves 4

16   to 18 fresh jumbo shrimp
    in their shells
    Kosher salt
    Cracked black pepper
½   cup olive oil
1   tablespoon diced shallots
1   teaspoon minced garlic
1   cup Chardonnay wine
1   26-ounce jar tomato-base
    pasta sauce (any flavor)
1½   cups crumbled fresh feta cheese
3   tablespoons unsalted
    butter, cut up
1   tablespoon chopped
    fresh flat-leaf parsley

1. Preheat the oven to 350°F. Clean shrimp, removing shells; use tip of sharp knife to remove veins (see photo at left). Season shrimp on both sides with salt and pepper. In a medium sauté pan heat 6 tablespoons of the olive oil over medium to high heat. Add shrimp to hot oil. Add shallots and garlic. Stir in Chardonnay. Sauté shrimp about 4 minutes or until done and orange in color, turning once. Transfer mixture to a 2-quart casserole, arranging shrimp in a single layer.

2. In a small saucepan heat pasta sauce until bubbly. Spoon pasta sauce over shrimp. Top with feta cheese and butter. Bake just until heated through. Remove casserole from oven. Drizzle with the remaining 2 tablespoons olive oil. Sprinkle with parsley.

get in
AND *G*ET OUT

Let's do lunch! My fresh takes on soups, salads, and sandwiches will hit the spot any time. – G

You've had a busy morning and can't believe it's already time for lunch. But you're on a deadline so you don't want to stop and eat—and you don't want to fill up too much and feel sleepy afterward. So you push through, which causes your brain to work harder because you're hungry, which means you're not working at full capacity, which means you're not doing the best job you can do! This chapter features fast recipes for soups, salads, and sandwiches that will give you the energy you need to knock out that project, shine for the boss, and maybe even get a raise.

CHECK OUT THESE PAGES FOR FUN AND FLAVORFUL WAYS TO GET IN, GET OUT, AND GET BACK TO WORK.

BLACKENED STEAK WITH PASTA AND MUSHROOMS SOUP

start to finish: 35 minutes / serves 6

12 ounces beef skirt steak,
    cut into 12 portions
1 to 2 teaspoons G's
    Blackening Spice
1 cup fresh shiitake mushrooms
2 teaspoons olive oil
2 cloves garlic, smashed
4 cups beef stock
2 cups chicken stock
1 cup vegetable stock
2 ounces dried angel hair pasta,
    broken in half
3 scallions, bias-cut into
    ¼-inch-long pieces

1. Cut three portions of the beef into small cubes; season with Blackening Spice. Set aside. Remove and discard stems from mushrooms. Thinly slice mushrooms; set aside.

2. In a medium saucepan heat olive oil over medium heat. Reduce heat to low. Add garlic and cubed skirt steak; sauté for 3 minutes. Add mushrooms, beef stock, chicken stock, and vegetable stock. Cook for 5 minutes.

3. Add angel hair pasta and the remaining nine portions skirt steak. Cook about 10 minutes or until pasta is tender. Stir in scallions.

G'S NOTE: --
G'S BLACKENING SPICE IS A TONGUE-TINGLING CAJUN SEASONING THAT'S GOOD ON STEAK, CHICKEN, OR FISH. LOOK FOR IT AT WWW.CHEFGARVIN.COM.

BEEF, CHICKEN, AND BROCCOLI

start to finish: 30 minutes / serves 6

12 ounces beef sirloin tips, thinly sliced
¼ teaspoon salt
¼ teaspoon G's Salt Seasoning
¼ teaspoon black pepper
3 tablespoons vegetable oil
12 ounces boneless, skinless chicken breast, thinly sliced
2 large bunches fresh broccoli, cut into florets
3 cloves garlic, chopped
2 small shallots, chopped
1 teaspoon cornstarch
1 teaspoon water
⅓ cup cold water
3 tablespoons soy sauce
Hot cooked white or brown rice

1. In a medium bowl combine beef, salt, Salt Seasoning, and pepper, tossing to coat meat. In a wok or large nonstick sauté pan heat 2 tablespoons of the vegetable oil over medium-high heat until hot but not smoking. Add beef and chicken. Stir-fry about 3 minutes or until cooked through. Using a slotted spoon transfer to a clean bowl; cover loosely with foil. Keep warm.

2. Add the remaining 1 tablespoon vegetable oil to wok or sauté pan. Add broccoli, garlic, and shallots. Stir-fry over medium-high heat about 2 minutes or just until broccoli is tender and garlic is a pale golden brown.

3. In a small bowl combine cornstarch and the 1 teaspoon water; set aside. Add the ⅓ cup water and the soy sauce to wok or sauté pan; bring mixture to a boil. Return beef and chicken to wok. Add cornstarch mixture. Cook and stir about 3 minutes or until sauce is thickened. Serve over hot cooked rice.

WHITE BEAN AND CRISPY PANCETTA SOUP

prep: 10 minutes / cook: 22 minutes / serves 6

1 cup diced pancetta
2 15- to 16-ounce cans Great Northern beans or cannellini beans (white kidney beans), rinsed and drained
1 shallot, diced
4 cups chicken stock
2 cups heavy cream, reduced
Kosher salt
Cracked white pepper

1. Heat a medium saucepan over medium heat. Add pancetta; sauté for 10 to 12 minutes or until pancetta is crispy. Drain off fat. Add beans and shallot to saucepan; sweat for 2 minutes, stirring occasionally.

2. Add chicken stock; bring to a boil. Reduce heat; simmer for 10 minutes. Stir in cream. Season to taste with salt and pepper. Heat through but do not boil.

SUPER SIMPLE HAM CALZONES

prep: 20 minutes / bake: 10 minutes / makes 4 calzones

Nonstick cooking spray
1 tablespoon olive oil
1 cup sliced fresh mushrooms
1 cup part-skim ricotta cheese
1 cup shredded mozzarella cheese
4 ounces finely chopped
   cooked ham
2 teaspoons chopped
   fresh oregano
1 teaspoon granulated garlic
4 refrigerated large flaky biscuits
1 egg yolk
2 tablespoons water

1. Preheat oven to 400°F. Spray a baking sheet with nonstick cooking spray; set aside. In a medium sauté pan heat olive oil over medium-high heat. Add mushrooms; sauté about 2 minutes or until mushrooms are soft. Drain on paper towels to soak up excess liquid; set aside.

2. For filling, in a bowl combine mushrooms, ricotta cheese, mozzarella cheese, ham, oregano, and granulated garlic.

3. Place each biscuit between two sheets of waxed paper. Roll each from center to edge to form a 6-inch circle (see photo below). Divide filling among circles, placing filling on half of each circle. Moisten edges of circles slightly with water. Fold over the sides of the circles without filling turnover-style, forming calzones. Use the tines of a fork to seal edges.

4. In a small bowl combine egg yolk and water. Brush egg mixture on tops of calzones. Place calzones on prepared baking sheet. Bake for 10 to 12 minutes or until golden brown.

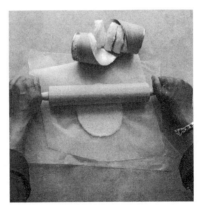

G'S NOTE: BEFORE BAKING, POKE THE TOP OF EACH CALZONE A FEW TIMES WITH THE TINES OF A FORK SO THE STEAM CAN ESCAPE.

KICKED-UP GRILLED CHEESE
WITH PROSCIUTTO AND SUN-DRIED TOMATOES

start to finish: 20 minutes / makes 4 sandwiches

8 slices wheat, white or potato bread

2 tablespoons Dijon mustard

8 slices Gruyère cheese

1 pound thinly sliced prosciutto

8 ounces sun-dried tomatoes (not in oil)

¼ cup (½ stick) unsalted butter, softened

Potato chips or kettle chips

1. Spread four of the bread slices with a light coating of Dijon mustard. Place bread slices, mustard sides up, on a flat surface. Top each with one slice of the Gruyère cheese. Divide prosciutto and sun-dried tomatoes among bread slices. Top each stack with another slice of the Gruyère cheese and another slice of the bread. Lightly spread outsides of the sandwiches with butter.

2. Heat a large skillet over medium heat. Place two of the sandwiches in skillet. Cook for 4 to 6 minutes or until golden brown, turning once. Repeat with the remaining two sandwiches. Serve with potato chips or kettle chips.

SMOKED HAM-AND-GRUYÈRE SANDWICHES

prep: 10 minutes / cook: 6 minutes per sandwich / makes 2 sandwiches

8 fresh basil leaves, diced

2 tablespoons mayonnaise

2 teaspoons lemon juice

4 slices potato bread

16 to 20 thin slices smoked ham (such as Black Forest)

6 slices Gruyère cheese

2 tablespoons unsalted butter

Kettle chips

1. In a small bowl combine basil, mayonnaise, and lemon juice. Spread one side of each bread slice with some of the mayonnaise mixture.

2. Place two bread slices, mayonnaise sides up, on a flat surface. Divide ham slices between the two bread slices. Top each with three slices Gruyère cheese. Add remaining two bread slices, mayonnaise sides down.

3. In a small sauté pan melt 1½ teaspoons of the butter over low heat. Add one sandwich; toast for 3 minutes. Turn sandwich. Add 1½ teaspoons more butter; toast for 3 minutes more. Set sandwich aside. Repeat with remaining sandwich and butter. Cut sandwiches in half diagonally. Serve with kettle chips.

SEE PHOTO, PAGE 156

GRILLED VEGGIES, SOPRESSATA, AND GOAT CHEESE SANDWICHES

start to finish: 35 minutes / makes 4 sandwiches

2	medium eggplants, peeled and cut into ¼-inch-thick slices
2	red bell peppers, seeded and cut into quarters
2	yellow bell peppers, seeded and cut into quarters
1	large red onion, cut into ¼-inch-thick rings
3	tablespoons olive oil
2	cloves garlic, diced
	Salt
	Freshly ground black pepper
4	6-inch baguettes, halved horizontally
1½	pounds thinly sliced sopressata
12	fresh basil leaves
1	cup crumbled goat cheese

1. Preheat oven to 300°F. In a bowl combine eggplant, bell peppers, and onion. Toss with 2 tablespoons of the olive oil. Mix in garlic. Season with salt and black pepper.
2. Heat a grill pan over medium-high heat. Add veggies to grill pan; cook for 3 minutes (work in batches, if necessary). Turn veggies over; cook for 4 to 5 minutes more or until veggies are tender. Remove veggies from grill pan; set aside.
3. Drizzle baguette bottoms with the remaining 1 tablespoon olive oil. Place baguette halves, cut sides up, on a baking sheet. Bake for 3 to 4 minutes or until lightly toasted. Remove from oven.
4. To make sandwiches, divide sopressata among baguette bottoms. Top with veggies. Top each sandwich with three basil leaves and some of the goat cheese. Add baguette tops. Serve warm.

SPICY LAMB KABOBS WITH MINTED NECTARINE SALSA

prep: 25 minutes / marinate: 30 minutes to 24 hours / grill: 8 minutes / serves 4

2 teaspoons olive oil
2 teaspoons finely grated
   lemon zest
1½ teaspoons finely grated lime zest
1 teaspoon coriander seeds,
   finely crushed
1 clove garlic, crushed
   Kosher salt
   Coarsely ground black pepper
1 pound lean lamb, cut into
   2-inch cubes
4 to 6 fresh red chile peppers,
   halved and seeded*
   Nectarine Salsa

1. For marinade, in large bowl combine olive oil, lemon zest, lime zest, coriander seeds, and garlic. Season with salt and black pepper. Add lamb; toss with marinade to coat. Cover and marinate in the refrigerator for at least 30 minutes or up to 24 hours.

2. Thread lamb and chile pepper pieces onto four 8- to 10-inch skewers. (If using wooden skewers, soak them in cold water for at least 30 minutes before threading with meat and chile pepper pieces to prevent burning when grilling.) Place kabobs on the grill rack of an uncovered grill directly over medium coals. Grill for 8 to 12 minutes or until done (160°F), turning once. Serve skewers with Nectarine Salsa and garlic bread.

NECTARINE SALSA: In a large bowl combine 3 ripe nectarines, halved, pitted, and diced; 1 small red onion, finely chopped; 3 tablespoons chopped fresh mint; and 2 tablespoons lime juice.

*NOTE: Because chile peppers contain volatile oils that can burn your skin and eyes, avoid direct contact with them as much as possible. When working with chile peppers, wear plastic or rubber gloves. If your bare hands do touch the peppers, wash your hands and nails well with soap and warm water.

G'S NOTES:----------------------------------
SPRING ONIONS ARE YOUNG FRESH ONIONS THAT ARE
LARGER THAN SCALLIONS. THEY'RE GREAT TO USE
WHEN YOU CAN FIND THEM. IF THEY'RE OUT OF SEASON,
SCALLIONS WILL DO.

SUPER SIMPLE CHICKEN CAESAR SALAD

prep: 15 minutes / marinate: 2 to 8 hours / cook: 8 minutes / serves 4

4   boneless, skinless
       chicken breast halves
1½   cups creamy Caesar
       salad dressing
½   cup chopped bacon
1   10-ounce package romaine
       lettuce hearts, torn into
       bite-size pieces
1   cup garlic croutons
½   cup grated Parmesan cheese

1. Place chicken breast halves in a resealable plastic bag set in a shallow dish. Pour ½ cup of the salad dressing over chicken; seal bag. Marinate in the refrigerator for at least 2 hours or up to 8 hours, turning bag occasionally.

2. In a skillet cook bacon until crispy. Drain bacon on paper towels; set aside. Drain chicken, discarding salad dressing. Grease a grill pan; heat over medium heat. Add chicken; cook for 8 to 12 minutes or until done (170°F), turning once. Remove chicken from grill pan; slice into bite-size strips.

3. In a large bowl combine romaine lettuce, croutons, and Parmesan cheese. Toss with the remaining 1 cup salad dressing. Divide among four salad plates. Divide chicken strips among plates; sprinkle with bacon. Serve immediately.

CHICKEN AND PENNE RIGATE WITH SNOW PEAS SOUP

start to finish: 30 minutes / serves 6

4   boneless, skinless chicken
       thighs, finely diced
       Kosher salt
       Ground white pepper
2   teaspoons olive oil
2   cloves garlic, smashed
6   cups chicken stock
2   cups water
1   cup dried penne rigate pasta
1½   cups fresh snow peas,
       cut on a bias

1. In a bowl season chicken with salt and white pepper. In medium saucepan heat olive oil over low heat. Add chicken and garlic; sweat for 5 minutes, stirring occasionally so chicken doesn't stick.

2. Add chicken stock and water; bring to a boil. Add penne rigate. Return to boiling; reduce heat. Simmer for 10 minutes. Add snow peas; simmer about 1 minute more or until pasta is tender.

TURKEY, CHEESE, AND PEPPER SANDWICHES

prep: 15 minutes / cook: 4 minutes / makes 4 sandwiches

2   tablespoons grated
    Parmesan cheese
1   tablespoon olive oil
8   slices sourdough bread
4   slices provolone cheese
4   ¼-inch-thick slices smoked turkey
½   cup roasted red pepper
    strips, drained
½   cup fresh baby arugula leaves
    Crushed red pepper
    Basil Mayonnaise (opposite)
2   tablespoons unsalted
    butter, softened

1. In small bowl combine Parmesan cheese and olive oil. Spread mixture on one side of each bread slice.

2. To assemble sandwiches, place four bread slices, cheese sides up, on a flat surface. Top each with some of the provolone cheese, turkey, red pepper strips, and arugula. Sprinkle each sandwich with crushed red pepper and top with Basil Mayonnaise. Top with remaining four bread slices, cheese sides down. Spread the outsides of sandwiches with butter.

3. Heat a panini grill or griddle over medium heat. Cook sandwiches for 4 to 6 minutes or until toasted and crisp, turning once.

PASTA E FAGIOLI WITH TURKEY SAUSAGE SOUP

prep: 30 minutes / cook: 20 minutes / serves 6

1   tablespoon olive oil
8   ounces ground uncooked
    turkey sausage
2   medium green and/or red bell
    peppers, seeded and diced
1   medium onion, chopped
6   cloves garlic, finely chopped
1   28-ounce can peeled plum
    tomatoes, drained, seeded,
    and chopped
10 fresh basil leaves, shredded
2   tablespoons chopped
    fresh parsley
2   19-ounce cans cannellini beans
    (white kidney beans), undrained
6   cups chicken stock
4   ounces dried mini penne pasta
    Kosher salt
    Black pepper
    Grated Parmesan cheese

1. In medium soup pot heat olive oil over medium heat. Add sausage; cook and stir until cooked through. Drain off fat. Add bell peppers, onion, and garlic; sauté until vegetables are soft and translucent. Add tomatoes, basil, and 1 tablespoon of the parsley. Cook about 10 minutes or until tomatoes release their juices.

2. Add undrained cannellini beans. Stir in chicken stock. Bring to a boil. Add penne; return to boiling. Cook about 8 to 10 minutes or until penne is al dente. Season with salt and black pepper.

3. Ladle into six soup bowls. Sprinkle each bowl with some of the remaining 1 tablespoon parsley and Parmesan cheese.

LEMON PEPPER CHICKEN SANDWICHES WITH
ARUGULA, ROASTED PEPPERS, AND HONEY-MUSTARD MAYO

prep: 15 minutes / marinate: 10 to 15 minutes / cook: 6 minutes / makes 2 sandwiches

½ teaspoon granulated garlic
1 teaspoon G's Lemon Pepper
    Seasoning
    Kosher salt
    Coarsely ground black pepper
1 teaspoon olive oil
2 6-ounce boneless, skinless
    chicken breast halves,
    halved horizontally
2 sourdough hoagie buns, split
2 tablespoons honey
2 tablespoons Dijon mustard
1 tablespoon mayonnaise
8 to 10 fresh arugula leaves
1 4-ounce jar roasted red
    peppers, drained

1. Preheat broiler. In a small bowl combine granulated garlic and Lemon Pepper Seasoning with salt and black pepper to taste. Stir in olive oil. Coat chicken slices with garlic mixture. Marinate in the refrigerator for 10 to 15 minutes.

2. Meanwhile, arrange hoagie buns, cut sides up, on broiler pan. Broil until lightly toasted. Remove from broiler. For honey-mustard mayo, in a small bowl combine honey, Dijon mustard, and mayonnaise. Spread cut sides of the buns with honey-mustard mayo; set aside.

3. Heat a medium nonstick sauté pan over medium-high heat. Add chicken pieces; cook for 6 to 8 minutes or until done, turning once. Remove from pan; set aside.

4. To make sandwiches, divide arugula leaves and roasted red peppers among bun bottoms. Top each with chicken and bun top.

G'S NOTES: --------------------------------
BASIL MAYONNAISE MAKES A QUICK, FLAVORFUL
TOPPER FOR SANDWICHES SUCH AS TURKEY, CHEESE,
AND PEPPER SANDWICHES (RECIPE OPPOSITE). IN
A FOOD PROCESSOR COMBINE 1 CUP MAYONNAISE,
5 TABLESPOONS CHOPPED FRESH BASIL, 1 TABLESPOON
CHOPPED GARLIC, 1 TEASPOON CHOPPED SHALLOT, AND
1 TABLESPOON LEMON JUICE. PULSE UNTIL SMOOTH.

FISH-AND-CHIPS SANDWICHES

start to finish: 40 minutes / makes 8 sandwiches

2　pounds skinless fresh cod
　　Kosher salt
　　Pinch cayenne pepper
1　egg
½　cup heavy cream
2　cups panko bread crumbs
　　Canola oil for frying
8　potato bread sandwich buns, split
½　cup tartar sauce
1　cup shredded lettuce
4　large tomatoes, sliced
1　large red onion, thinly sliced
　　Chopped fresh parsley
　　Kettle chips

1. Rinse fish; pat dry with paper towels. Cut into eight portions. Season fish with salt and cayenne pepper. For egg wash, in a bowl beat together egg and cream until well mixed. Place bread crumbs in a shallow bowl.

2. In large skillet heat ½ inch canola oil until hot (375°F). Dip fish portions in egg wash, then in bread crumbs (see photos below). Place half of the fish portions in hot oil. Cook about 8 minutes or until done and coating is golden brown, turning once. Drain on paper towels to absorb oil. Repeat with remaining fish.

3. To make sandwiches, spread bottom halves of sandwich buns with tartar sauce. Top bun bottoms with fish, lettuce, tomato, and onion. Sprinkle each sandwich with parsley. Add bun tops. Serve with kettle chips.

𝒢'S GOTTA-BE-QUICK TIP: ----------------

IF YOU FIND YOURSELF DOING A BETTER JOB GETTING THE COATING ON YOUR FINGERS THAN ON THE FISH, TRY THIS: USE ONE HAND FOR DIPPING THE FISH IN THE EGG WASH AND THE OTHER HAND FOR DIPPING IT IN THE CRUMBS.

POTATO-AND-GARLIC SOUP

start to finish: 35 minutes / serves 6

2   tablespoons olive oil
6   cloves garlic, smashed
1   shallot, chopped
4   potatoes, peeled and cut up
3   sprigs fresh rosemary
    Kosher salt
    Ground white pepper
4   cups chicken stock
4   cups water
2   cups heavy cream
1   cup milk

1. In a large saucepan heat olive oil over medium heat. Add garlic and shallot; sauté for 2 minutes. Add potatoes and rosemary. Season with salt and white pepper. Sweat for 4 minutes, stirring occasionally.

2. Add chicken stock, water, and 1 cup of the cream. Simmer about 15 minutes or until potatoes are soft. Blend half of the mixture in a food processor until smooth. Pour through a strainer; set aside strained mixture. Repeat with remaining potato mixture. Return all of the potato mixture to the saucepan.

3. Add the remaining 1 cup cream and the milk. Bring to a boil; check the seasoning. Serve immediately.

FRESH TUNA SALAD ON WHOLE WHEAT KAISER ROLLS

start to finish: 30 minutes / makes 2 sandwiches

2   6-ounce skinless fresh tuna fillets
1½   cups water
2   whole wheat kaiser rolls, split
½   cup mayonnaise
¼   cup finely diced red onion
1   teaspoon capers, drained
1   teaspoon granulated garlic
1   teaspoon grated lemon zest
½   teaspoon mayonnaise
     G's Salt Seasoning
     Coarsely ground black pepper
4   medium romaine lettuce leaves
2   plum tomatoes, thinly sliced

1. Preheat broiler. Rinse fish; pat dry with paper towels. Measure thickness of fish. In a large skillet bring the water to a boil. Add fish; return to boiling. Reduce heat; simmer for 4 to 6 minutes per ½-inch thickness of fish or until done. Remove fish from water; set aside to cool.

2. Meanwhile, arrange rolls, cut sides up, on unheated rack of a broiler pan. Broil 4 to 5 inches from heat for 1 to 2 minutes or until lightly toasted. Transfer rolls to a wire rack to cool.

3. In a medium bowl break fish into bite-size pieces. Fold in mayonnaise, red onion, capers, granulated garlic, lemon zest, and mayonnaise. Season with Salt Seasoning and pepper.

4. To serve, divide tuna mixture between roll bottoms. Add 2 lettuce leaves to each sandwich. Top each with tomato slices and a roll top.

MAKE-AHEAD DIRECTIONS: If you like, prepare the tuna salad up to 24 hours ahead. Cover and chill it in the refrigerator.

BLACK BEAN, TORTILLA, AND CHEDDAR SOUP

start to finish: 45 minutes / serves 6

4½ teaspoons olive oil
1   medium white onion, finely diced
1   tablespoon chopped garlic
1   tablespoon chopped shallots
¼   teaspoon chili powder
¼   teaspoon ground cumin
1   15-ounce can black beans,
    rinsed and drained
4   plum tomatoes, diced
1   cup frozen corn
1   6-ounce bag tortilla chips
3½ cups chicken stock
1   tablespoon chopped
    fresh cilantro
    Salt
    Black pepper
1   cup shredded cheddar cheese
    Sour cream
¼   cup chopped scallions
    Fresh chives
    Tortilla chips

1. In a medium stockpot heat olive oil over medium-high heat. Add onion, garlic, and shallots. Sauté until onions are soft. Stir in chili powder and cumin. Add black beans, tomatoes, and corn. Cook about 5 minutes more or until tomatoes start to get limp.

2. Break up tortilla chips in the bag. Add broken chips to mixture in stockpot, stirring to mix well. Add chicken stock. Bring to a boil; reduce heat. Simmer for 10 minutes. Stir in cilantro. Season to taste with salt and pepper. Cook about 10 minutes more or until beans start to get soft and pasty.

3. If desired, use an immersion blender to blend smooth. To finish, fold in cheddar cheese until completely melted. Ladle into six soup bowls. Top each serving with sour cream, scallions, chives, and additional tortilla chips.

SEE PHOTO, PAGE 44

G'S NOTES: ------------------------------

TO KICK THE FLAVOR OF THIS SOUP UP A NOTCH, USE PEPPER JACK CHEESE INSTEAD OF CHEDDAR CHEESE.

FRESH VEGETABLE SOUP

prep: 25 minutes / cook: 20 minutes / serves 12

1	tablespoon olive oil
2	cups diced peeled plum tomatoes
½	cup fresh corn cut off the cob
½	cup diced zucchini
½	cup diced yellow squash
½	of a medium onion, diced
2	cloves garlic, diced
	Kosher salt
2	tablespoons tomato paste
10	cups vegetable stock
8	ounces fresh baby spinach

1. In a large saucepan heat olive oil over medium heat. Add tomatoes, corn, zucchini, yellow squash, onion, and garlic. Season with salt. Sauté for 8 minutes.
2. Stir in tomato paste. Add vegetable stock. Bring to a boil; reduce heat. Simmer for 10 minutes. Add spinach. Check seasoning. Serve immediately.

SPICY CRAB-AND-CORN CHOWDER

prep: 25 minutes / cook: 35 minutes / serves 8

1	tablespoon olive oil
½	cup diced celery
½	cup chopped andouille sausage
¼	cup finely chopped onion
¼	cup finely chopped garlic
3	cups chicken stock
2	cups water
1	cup cubed potatoes
2	8¼- to 8¾-ounce cans cream-style corn
1	cup lump crabmeat
1	cup milk
1	cup heavy cream
	Kosher salt
	Black pepper
½	cup chopped scallions

1. In a medium stockpot heat olive oil over medium heat. Add celery, andouille sausage, onion, and garlic. Sauté about 5 minutes or until vegetables are soft.
2. Add chicken stock, water, and potatoes. Bring to a boil; reduce heat. Cover and simmer for 20 to 25 minutes or until potatoes are tender. Add corn, crabmeat, milk, and cream. Simmer for 10 minutes.
3. Season to taste with salt and pepper. Ladle into eight soup bowls. Top each serving with some of the scallions.

TOMATOES-AND-MOZZARELLA SALAD
WITH BALSAMIC VINAIGRETTE

start to finish: 25 minutes / serves 4

5   bias-cut baguette slices
1   tablespoon unsalted
      butter, softened
2   red heirloom tomatoes, sliced
      into small rounds
2   yellow heirloom tomatoes,
      sliced into small rounds
4   medium balls fresh mozzarella,
      cut into small rounds
3   cups fresh arugula leaves
1   cup fresh basil leaves
¼   cup balsamic vinaigrette
      salad dressing

1. Preheat oven to 425°F. Spread one side of each baguette slice with some of the butter. Arrange baguette slices, buttered sides up, on a baking sheet. Bake for 3 to 5 minutes or until lightly toasted. Remove from oven; set aside. Cut into bite-size pieces for croutons.

2. On a large platter arrange tomato and cheese slices alternately in a circle. In a bowl toss together arugula, basil, and balsamic vinaigrette. Serve greens mixture with tomato and cheese slices. Sprinkle with croutons.

SEE PHOTO, PAGE 46

BACON-AND-EGG SANDWICHES

start to finish: 25 minutes / makes 3 sandwiches

9   slices bacon
8   eggs
      Kosher salt
      Ground white pepper
      Unsalted butter
1   tablespoon olive oil
3   medium focaccia rolls or 4-inch
      pieces of French bread, split
12   fresh arugula leaves

1. Preheat oven to 300°F. In a large sauté pan cook bacon until crispy. Remove bacon from pan; drain on paper towels. Set bacon aside; discard bacon drippings. In a large bowl lightly beat eggs until combined; season with salt and pepper. Set aside.

2. In the same sauté pan heat 1 tablespoon butter and the olive oil over medium heat. As butter starts to melt, add egg mixture. Scramble eggs for 3 minutes. Add another 1 tablespoon of the butter. Cook eggs about 1 minute more or until eggs are cooked through but still slightly moist. Turn off the heat.

3. Spread cut sides of focaccia with 1½ teaspoons butter. Place focaccia halves, cut sides up, on a baking sheet; bake about 2 minutes or until lightly toasted. Remove from oven. Divide egg mixture among focaccia bottoms. Place three bacon slices and four arugula leaves on each sandwich; add focaccia tops. To serve, cut sandwiches in half.

CHEESY CAULIFLOWER SOUP

start to finish: 35 minutes / serves 12

Kosher salt
Black pepper
2 pounds fresh cauliflower, chopped
2 tablespoons unsalted butter
2 cups diced onion
2 tablespoons minced garlic
2 tablespoons all-purpose flour
10 cups chicken stock
2 cups heavy cream
1 cup shredded sharp cheddar cheese
Toasted garlic bread (optional)

1. In a large pot bring water to a boil; add salt and pepper. Add cauliflower; boil about 10 minutes or until tender.

2. Meanwhile, in a soup pot melt butter over medium heat. Add onion and garlic. Sauté about 5 minutes or until the onion and garlic are softened. Sprinkle flour into pot. Add about 1 cup of the chicken stock, a little at a time, continuing to stir so mixture does not become lumpy. Once you have approximately a cup of smooth, thick liquid, add the rest of the stock. Reduce heat to low and simmer.

3. Drain cauliflower and puree in a blender until creamy and smooth. Stir cauliflower into simmering stock mixture. Stir in cream. Whisk in cheddar cheese. Simmer for 5 minutes. If desired, serve with toasted garlic bread.

WORKIN' IT OUT

Eating what's good for you doesn't have to mean giving up the foods you love. You can eat guilt-free any time with my tasty and so, so simple recipes. — G

Here are some lighter, leaner recipes if you're hitting the gym (like me) or just want to eat a little better a couple of times a week. The biggest challenge I find is eating healthier while I'm traveling. On the road, it's all fast food and the same ho-hum options in hotel restaurants. So recently I decided that I would go old-school style and pack a lunch when I travel. It saves me money, and I can eat what I want and when I want. And the best thing is that eating healthier always makes me feel better.

YOU'LL SEE HOW COOKING LIGHTER

DOESN'T MEAN LESS FLAVOR.

SEARED BLACK PEPPER LAMB LOIN
WITH SAUTÉED SPINACH

start to finish: 35 minutes / serves 6

3 8-ounce pieces boneless
   lamb loin
   Kosher salt
   Cracked black pepper
6 tablespoons olive oil
2 tablespoons unsalted butter
1 tablespoon minced garlic
1 9-ounce package fresh spinach

1. Season lamb with salt. Press 3 tablespoons pepper onto surface of meat (see photo below). In a large sauté pan heat 4 tablespoons of the olive oil over medium heat. Add lamb; sear for 3 minutes. Turn lamb over; sear for 3 minutes more. Turn lamb over a third time; sear for 3 minutes. Turn lamb over again; sear about 3 minutes or until done (155°F). Remove meat from pan to a cutting board; cover meat with foil. Let stand for 15 minutes. Slice meat.

2. In the same sauté pan heat the remaining 2 tablespoons olive oil and the butter over medium heat until butter is melted. Stir in garlic; add spinach. Sauté just until spinach is wilted. Season with additional salt and pepper.

3. To serve, transfer spinach mixture to a serving platter. Arrange meat slices on top.

BLACKENED PORK CHOPS
WITH STEWED CHERRY TOMATOES AND BASIL

prep: 20 minutes / bake: 10 minutes / serves 4

4	6-ounce pork chops
	G's Blackening Spice
¼	cup olive oil
1½	cups red cherry tomatoes
1½	cups yellow cherry tomatoes
3	shallots, diced
1	tablespoon unsalted butter
12	to 14 fresh basil leaves

1. Preheat oven to 350°F. Season pork chops on both sides with Blackening Spice. In a large oven-going skillet heat 2 tablespoons of the olive oil. Add pork chops; cook for 10 minutes, turning once.

2. Add the remaining 2 tablespoons olive oil, the cherry tomatoes, shallots, and butter to skillet. Bake for 8 minutes; add basil. Bake for 2 to 4 minutes more or until chops are done (160°F). Transfer pork chops to four dinner plates. Top each pork chop with some of the tomato mixture.

SEE PHOTO, PAGE 48

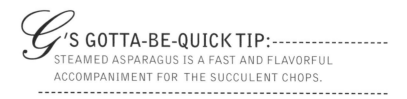

G'S GOTTA-BE-QUICK TIP: ----------------
STEAMED ASPARAGUS IS A FAST AND FLAVORFUL
ACCOMPANIMENT FOR THE SUCCULENT CHOPS.

CHICKEN SALAD

prep: 15 minutes / grill: 12 minutes / serves 6

⅓ cup olive oil

3 tablespoons red wine vinegar

2 tablespoons chopped shallots

2 cloves garlic, minced

4 skinless, boneless chicken
     breast halves

2 cloves garlic, peeled and halved
    Salt
    Black pepper

1 8- to 10-ounce package torn
     mixed greens

18 jumbo ripe olives

2 navel oranges, peeled and sliced

1. For dressing, in a screw-top jar combine olive oil, red wine vinegar, shallots, the minced garlic, ½ teaspoon salt, and ½ teaspoon pepper. Cover and shake well. Set aside.

2. Rub chicken with halved garlic cloves. Season chicken with additional salt and pepper. Place chicken on rack of an uncovered grill directly over medium coals. Grill for 12 to 15 minutes or until done (170°F), turning once. (Or preheat broiler. Place chicken on the unheated rack of a broiler pan. Broil 4 to 5 inches from heat for 12 to 15 minutes or until done [170°F], turning once.) Transfer chicken to a cutting board; let cool. Chop or pull chicken into bite-size pieces.

3. Meanwhile, arrange greens, olives, and oranges on six salad plates. Divide chicken among salad plates. Shake salad dressing; drizzle over salads.

G'S GOTTA-BE-QUICK TIP:------------------
IF YOU'RE SHORT ON TIME, PICK UP A ROASTED CHICKEN
AT YOUR SUPERMARKET'S DELI COUNTER INSTEAD OF
GRILLING THE CHICKEN.

VERMICELLI WITH SAUTÉED CABBAGE, CARROTS, AND CHICKEN IN ASIAN DRESSING

start to finish: 30 minutes / serves 4

Olive oil

8 ounces dried vermicelli
   or linguine pasta

1 tablespoon lower-sodium
   soy sauce

1 teaspoon lemon juice

1 teaspoon chopped garlic

1 teaspoon chopped fresh ginger

1 teaspoon chopped fresh tarragon

8 ounces boneless, skinless
   chicken breasts, sliced

1 cup shredded cabbage

½ cup sliced carrots

½ cup red bell pepper cut in short
   julienne strips

   Kosher salt

   Coarsely ground black pepper

1. In a large pot bring water to a boil; add 1½ teaspoons olive oil. Add vermicelli; cook according to package directions. Drain; return to hot pot. Keep warm.

2. For dressing, in a screw-top jar combine soy sauce, 1 tablespoon olive oil, lemon juice, garlic, ginger, and tarragon. Cover and shake well; set aside.

3. In a large sauté pan heat 1 tablespoon olive oil. Add chicken to hot oil; sauté for 3 to 4 minutes or until done. Remove chicken from pan; set aside. Add cabbage, carrots, and bell pepper to hot pan; sauté just until cabbage wilts. Return chicken to pan. Shake dressing well; stir into pan. In a bowl combine chicken mixture with vermicelli, tossing to coat. Season to taste with salt and pepper.

SEE PHOTO, PAGE 158

HERB GARDEN CHICKEN BREASTS

prep: 15 minutes / broil: 12 minutes / serves 4

4 boneless, skinless
   chicken breast halves

   Salt

   Black pepper

1 tablespoon garlic powder

1 tablespoon onion powder

¼ cup chicken stock

2 tablespoons chopped shallots

1 tablespoon lime juice

2 cloves garlic, minced

1 teaspoon chopped
   fresh rosemary

   Hot cooked brown rice

   Hot cooked broccoli

1. Preheat broiler. Season chicken with salt and pepper; sprinkle with garlic powder and onion powder. Place chicken on the unheated rack of a broiler pan. Broil 4 to 5 inches from heat for 12 to 15 minutes or until done (170°F), turning once.

2. For herb sauce, in a small skillet combine chicken stock, shallots, lime juice, garlic, and rosemary. Heat over medium heat about 30 seconds or until mixture is warm.

3. To serve, slice chicken; arrange on four dinner plates. Drizzle with herb sauce. Serve with hot cooked brown rice and broccoli.

CHICKEN-AND-RICE SOUP

prep: 25 minutes / cook: 20 minutes / serves 8

1   tablespoon olive oil
1   large onion, diced
2   stalks celery, chopped
½   cup diced carrots
2   cloves garlic, minced
7   cups chicken stock
1   pound cooked boneless,
        skinless chicken breast,
        diced into ½-inch cubes
1   cup frozen peas
1   cup cooked rice
      Kosher salt
      Black pepper

1. In a large stockpot heat olive oil over medium heat. Add onion, celery, carrots, and garlic; sauté about 5 minutes or until vegetables are tender.

2. Add chicken stock; bring to a boil. Reduce heat. Stir in chicken, peas, and rice; cook until peas are tender. Season to taste with salt and pepper.

G'S GOTTA-BE-QUICK TIP:

INSTEAD OF USING FRESH CARROTS AND FROZEN PEAS IN THIS RECIPE, YOU CAN STIR IN 1½ CUPS FROZEN PEAS AND CARROTS ALONG WITH THE CHICKEN AND RICE.

GRILLED CHICKEN, PINEAPPLE, AND TURKEY BACON WITH TROPICAL DRESSING OVER MESCLUN

prep: 20 minutes / cook: 17 minutes / serves 4

4 slices turkey bacon

2 6-ounce boneless, skinless chicken breast halves

   Kosher salt

   Coarsely ground black pepper

2 tablespoons olive oil

½ of a medium pineapple, cleaned and sliced

1 5- to 8-ounce package mesclun greens

   Tropical Dressing

1. In a medium sauté pan cook bacon over medium heat until crispy. Drain bacon on paper towels. Crumble; set aside.

2. Place chicken in a bowl. Season with salt and pepper. Drizzle with 1 tablespoon of the olive oil. Place pineapple in a bowl; drizzle with the remaining 1 tablespoon olive oil. Heat a grill pan over medium-high heat; add chicken. Cook for 12 to 15 minutes or until chicken is done (170°F), turning once. Remove chicken from grill pan to a cutting board; set aside. Add pineapple to grill pan; cook for 5 to 8 minutes or until brown and fragrant, turning once. Remove from grill pan; set aside. Slice chicken.

3. To serve, arrange greens on four salad plates. Top each with chicken and pineapple. Sprinkle bacon over salads. Drizzle salads with Tropical Dressing.

TROPICAL DRESSING: In a bowl whisk together ¼ cup mayonnaise, 2 tablespoons orange juice, 2 tablespoons pineapple juice, 2 tablespoons mango nectar, 1 tablespoon honey, ½ teaspoon dry mustard, ½ teaspoon paprika, ½ teaspoon poppy seeds, ¼ teaspoon garlic powder, a dash ground ginger, and a pinch kosher salt.

TOMATO, TURKEY, AND CHEESE FRITTATA

start to finish: 35 minutes / serves 6

2 tablespoons olive oil
2 medium onions, thinly sliced
1 14½-ounce can Italian-style
     stewed tomatoes, undrained
6 eggs, beaten
½ cup chopped cooked turkey
½ cup chopped fresh basil
3 tablespoons grated
     Parmesan cheese
¼ teaspoon salt
⅛ teaspoon black pepper

1. Preheat broiler. In a large broilerproof skillet heat olive oil over medium heat. Add onions; sauté for 8 to 10 minutes or until onions are golden but not brown. Add undrained tomatoes; cook for 5 minutes more, stirring frequently.

2. In a bowl combine eggs, turkey, basil, Parmesan cheese, salt, and pepper. Turn heat under skillet to the lowest setting. Add egg mixture to skillet, stirring to combine with the onions and tomatoes. As mixture sets, run a spatula around the skillet edge, lifting egg mixture so uncooked portion flows underneath. Continue cooking and lifting edges until egg mixture is almost set (surface will be moist).

3. Broil for 1 to 2 minutes or just until the eggs on the surface have set.

HALIBUT WITH SAUTÉED TOMATOES, GARLIC, AND ONION

start to finish: 20 minutes / serves 4

4	6-ounce pieces skinless fresh halibut fillet
	Salt
	Black pepper
6	tablespoons olive oil
2	cups canned plum tomatoes
1	large onion, sliced
6	cloves garlic, smashed
	Hot cooked rice

1. Rinse fish; pat dry with paper towels. Bias-cut each fish piece into three portions. Season with salt and pepper.

2. In a large sauté pan heat 4 tablespoons of the olive oil over medium heat. Add tomatoes, onion, and garlic; sauté for 3 minutes. Move tomato mixture to center of pan.

3. Add the remaining 2 tablespoons olive oil to pan; place fish in pan around the tomatoes. Cover; simmer for 6 to 8 minutes or until done. Serve over hot cooked rice.

BAKED RED SNAPPER WITH BEAN-AND-SPINACH RAGOÛT

start to finish: 30 minutes / serves 6

12	slices prosciutto
¼	cup olive oil
2	medium shallots, diced
2	15- to 16-ounce cans cannellini beans (white kidney beans), Great Northern beans, or navy beans, rinsed and drained
6	cups chicken stock
	Kosher salt
	Cracked white pepper
6	6-ounce fresh red snapper fillets with skin
1	9-ounce package fresh spinach
½	of a medium cucumber, peeled and diced

1. Preheat oven to 400°F. Arrange prosciutto on a baking sheet; bake for 6 to 8 minutes or until fat turns golden and meat darkens slightly. Drain on paper towels (prosciutto will crisp as it cools). When cool, crumble prosciutto; set aside. Increase oven temperature to 450°F.

2. For bean ragoût, in a large saucepan heat 2 tablespoons of the olive oil; add shallots. Sauté until shallots are soft. Drain off fat. Add the beans to the saucepan. Sauté for 2 minutes. Add chicken stock. Season with salt and pepper. Bring to a boil; reduce heat. Simmer for 5 minutes; keep warm.

3. Meanwhile, rinse fish; pat dry with paper towels. Sprinkle fish with salt and pepper. In a large oven-going skillet heat the remaining 2 tablespoons olive oil; add fish. Cook for 3 minutes; turn fish. Bake in 450°F oven about 3 minutes or until done.

4. To serve, stir spinach and crumbled prosciutto into bean ragoût. Transfer bean ragoût to a serving platter. Top with fish; sprinkle with cucumber.

PEPPERED SHRIMP WRAPS

start to finish: 35 minutes / serves 2

8 ounces fresh medium shrimp
   in their shells
2 teaspoons olive oil
1 tablespoon chopped garlic
3 tablespoons lemon juice
1 tablespoon vermouth
1 teaspoon black pepper
   Kosher salt
1 cup shredded lettuce
1 medium tomato, diced
2 tablespoons red bell pepper cut in
   short julienne strips
2 tablespoons green bell pepper
   cut in short julienne strips
2 tablespoons red onion cut in
   short julienne strips
2 tablespoons scallions, chopped
8 black olives, sliced
2 8-inch flour tortillas

1. Clean shrimp, removing shells; use tip of sharp knife to remove veins. Pat dry with paper towels; set aside. In a medium sauté pan heat 1 teaspoon of the olive oil. Add garlic; sauté for 2 to 3 minutes. Remove pan from heat; stir in lemon juice, vermouth, and black pepper. Season with salt. Add shrimp. Return to heat; cook, stirring constantly, about 1 minute or until shrimp are done and firm to the touch. Remove from heat; cool.

2. In a large bowl combine lettuce, tomato, bell peppers, red onion, scallions, olives, and the remaining 1 teaspoon olive oil. Add shrimp mixture; toss to combine. Divide mixture between tortillas. Wrap to serve.

SEE PHOTO, PAGE 41

G'S NOTE: --------------------------------------
IF YOU LIKE, CHOP SOME FRESH HERBS AND STIR THEM
INTO LIGHT MAYONNAISE TO SERVE AS A DIPPING
SAUCE FOR THE WRAPS.

HALIBUT EN PAPILLOTE

prep: 25 minutes / bake: 15 minutes / serves 4

Olive oil nonstick cooking spray
4 8-ounce skinless fresh
   halibut fillets
   Sea salt
   Freshly ground black pepper
1 cup sliced red onion
1 cup carrots cut in
   short julienne strips
1 cup zucchini cut in
   short julienne strips
1 cup red bell pepper cut
   in short julienne strips
½ cup peeled and sliced parsnips
¼ cup lemon juice
24 mussels, cleaned and debearded
   (see photo below) (optional)
¼ cup Chardonnay wine
4 teaspoons chopped garlic
4 sprigs fresh thyme

1. Preheat oven to 400°F. Fold four 36×15-inch sheets heavy foil in half crosswise to form 18×15-inch rectangles. Working from the folded side of each rectangle, cut a half-heart shape so the fold runs through the center of the heart. Open each heart shape and coat with olive oil cooking spray.

2. Rinse fish; pat dry with paper towels. Season fish with salt and black pepper. In a large bowl combine red onion, carrots, zucchini, bell pepper, parsnips, and lemon juice. Divide the vegetable mixture among the foil hearts, mounding the vegetables in the center of one half of each heart. Top each mound of vegetables with a piece of fish. If desired, add six mussels to each mound. Top each mound with 1 tablespoon of the wine, 1 teaspoon of the garlic, and one thyme sprig.

3. To close each pouch, fold the second side of the foil over fish and vegetables. Fold the bottom edge over the top edge, folding and pleating until the pouch is sealed. If desired, twist the point of the heart to secure the seal. Place pouches on a large baking sheet. Bake for 15 to 20 minutes or until fish is done.

4. To serve, place a pouch on each of four dinner plates. Using a paring knife, cut an "X" in the top of each pouch. Fold back the foil carefully to avoid built-up steam as you open each pouch. (Or if desired, remove fish and vegetables from foil pouches and transfer to dinner plates.)

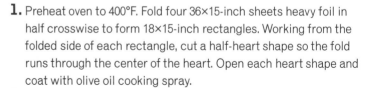

G'S NOTE:
IF YOU LIKE, YOU CAN USE PARCHMENT PAPER INSTEAD OF FOIL THE WAY THE PROS DO. LOOK FOR IT IN LARGE SUPERMARKETS NEAR THE FOIL.

GRILLED SALMON SALAD WITH POTATOES, GREEN BEANS, AND MESCLUN

prep: 15 minutes / cook: 35 minutes / serves 4

Kosher salt

8   red bee potatoes or other small red-skin potatoes, quartered

1½ cups fresh green beans

2   6-ounce pieces skinless fresh salmon fillets
    Cracked white pepper

1   5- to 8-ounce package mesclun greens

2   whole lemons, halved

¼   cup olive oil

1. In a large pot bring water to a boil; add salt. Add potatoes; return to boiling. Reduce heat; simmer, covered, for 10 minutes. Add green beans; cover and cook about 10 minutes more or until potatoes and beans are tender. Drain vegetables; set aside.

2. Rinse fish; pat dry with paper towels. Measure thickness of fish. Season fish with salt and white pepper. Grease a grill pan; heat over medium heat. Add fish; cook for 4 to 6 minutes per ½-inch thickness of fish or until done, turning once. Remove fish to a cutting board; break into bite-size pieces.

3. To serve, arrange greens on a large platter. Top with fish, potatoes, and beans. Squeeze juice from lemon halves over fish. Drizzle fish with olive oil; sprinkle with additional salt and white pepper.

SHRIMP SALAD

prep: 25 minutes / chill: 2 to 24 hours / serves 8

3   ounces dried rotini or other spiral pasta

2½ cups frozen cooked shrimp, thawed

2   cups fresh broccoli florets

⅓   cup chopped green bell pepper

⅓   cup chopped red bell pepper

⅓   cup chopped yellow bell pepper

⅓   cup sliced scallions

½   cup fat-free Italian salad dressing

¼   cup fat-free mayonnaise
    G's Garlic Salt
    G's Salt Seasoning
    Black pepper

1. In a medium pot bring water to a boil. Add rotini; cook according to package directions. Drain; rinse with cold water. Drain again.

2. In a bowl combine cooked pasta, shrimp, broccoli, bell peppers, and scallions.

3. In another bowl combine Italian salad dressing and mayonnaise. Pour over shrimp mixture, tossing to coat. Season to taste with Garlic Salt, Salt Seasoning, and black pepper. Cover and chill for at least 2 hours or up to 24 hours.

ASPARAGUS PASTA PRIMAVERA

start to finish: 25 minutes / serves 6

2 pounds fresh asparagus,
   tough bottoms removed
1 16-ounce package dried linguine
   pasta
¼ cup olive oil
½ cup diced red bell pepper
2 tablespoons chopped garlic
2 tablespoons chopped shallots
2 tablespoons Italian seasoning
1½ teaspoons grated lemon zest
   Salt
   Black pepper
¼ cup pine nuts, toasted
3 tablespoons chopped
   fresh parsley

1. Slice 3-inch-long pieces from the tips of the asparagus spears. Slice the remaining stalks diagonally into bite-size pieces. In a large stockpot bring water to a boil; add asparagus. Return to boiling; cook for 3 to 4 minutes or until asparagus is partially tender. Using a slotted spoon, remove asparagus to a bowl; set aside.

2. Return water to a boil. Add linguine; cook according to package directions.

3. Meanwhile, in a wide skillet heat 2 tablespoons of the olive oil over low heat. Add bell pepper, garlic, shallots, Italian seasoning, and lemon zest. Season with salt and black pepper. Sauté until bell pepper is soft. Add asparagus to the skillet. Sauté until asparagus is tender. Drain pasta, allowing some water to cling to the strands. Add pasta, the remaining 2 tablespoons olive oil, pine nuts, and parsley to skillet, tossing to coat pasta. Season with additional black pepper.

G'S NOTE: TO TOAST PINE NUTS, IN A SMALL DRY SKILLET HEAT PINE NUTS OVER MEDIUM HEAT, STIRRING FREQUENTLY, UNTIL GOLDEN BROWN.

QUICK-AND-TASTY GREAT NORTHERN BEAN SOUP

start to finish: 30 minutes / serves 6

1   tablespoon olive oil
1   medium onion, chopped
2   medium shallots, minced
2   cloves garlic, minced
2   15-ounce cans Great Northern
      beans, rinsed and drained
3½ cups chicken stock
1   15¼-ounce can whole
      kernel corn, drained
1   14½-ounce can diced
      tomatoes with basil, garlic,
      and oregano, undrained
1   teaspoon balsamic vinegar
½   teaspoon dried thyme
½   teaspoon dried basil
½   teaspoon cumin
2   bay leaves

1. In a large soup pot heat olive oil over medium heat; sauté onion, shallots, and garlic in hot oil about 5 minutes or until onion and shallots are soft.

2. Stir in beans, chicken stock, corn, undrained tomatoes, balsamic vinegar, thyme, basil, cumin, and bay leaves. Bring to a boil; reduce heat. Cover and simmer for 8 to 10 minutes or until heated through and desired consistency, stirring frequently. Remove bay leaves.

ALL THE FIXINGS

Who says eating veggies can't be cool? My latest flavor combos are terrific and come to the table in no time. – G

It doesn't matter how much (or how little) you say you're gonna eat because it always changes when the sides start to go down the table. You just can't help yourself—and why should you? One of the coolest things about sides is that they get the whole family involved, picking and fixing their favorites. To lighten your load in the kitchen, have guests bring their favorite sides to your next big meal. Not only do you get to enjoy lots of great veggies and potatoes, but you can rest assured that you'll get clean-up help because guests never want to leave their dishes.

GREAT SIDES ARE A REFLECTION OF A GREAT FAMILY. MANY AND ALL ARE WELCOME.

BEET SALAD

prep: 15 minutes / cook: 1 hour / serves 8

2 pounds fresh beets (about 8),
   peeled and cubed
1 cup water
¾ cup packed brown sugar
½ cup orange juice
½ cup pineapple juice
⅓ cup balsamic vinegar
2 tablespoons unsalted butter
8 ounces crumbled goat cheese
2 cups torn mixed greens
¼ cup pine nuts, toasted
   Balsamic vinegar

1. In a large saucepan combine beets, the water, brown sugar, orange juice, pineapple juice, the ⅓ cup balsamic vinegar, and the butter. Bring to a boil; reduce heat to medium-low. Simmer, uncovered, about 1 hour or until beets are tender and most of the liquid has boiled away. Remove from heat; cool.
2. To serve, divide beet mixture among eight salad plates. Sprinkle each serving with goat cheese; top with greens. Sprinkle with pine nuts. Drizzle with additional balsamic vinegar.

SEE PHOTO, PAGE 40

LIMA BEANS

start to finish: 20 minutes / serves 6

2 cups vegetable stock
1 16-ounce package frozen
   baby lima beans
1 tablespoon minced garlic
1 tablespoon chopped shallots
¼ cup white wine
½ to ¾ cup heavy cream
1½ to 2 tablespoons unsalted butter
   Salt
   Black pepper

1. In a large saucepan bring vegetable stock to a boil; add lima beans. Return to boiling; reduce heat. Simmer for 5 to 7 minutes or just until beans are tender. Stir in garlic and shallots. Add wine; simmer for 5 to 7 minutes more or just until mixture starts to thicken.
2. Stir in cream and butter; heat until mixture is thickened and bubbly. Season to taste with salt and pepper.

STRING BEANS WITH GARLIC AND ALMONDS

start to finish: 35 minutes / serves 4

3	tablespoons unsalted butter
1	teaspoon olive oil
⅓	cup sliced almonds
8	ounces fresh green beans, trimmed
1	cup cubed potatoes
1	tablespoon chopped shallots
2	teaspoons minced garlic
½	teaspoon kosher salt
½	cup vegetable stock
½	teaspoon freshly ground black pepper

1. In a large sauté pan melt 2 tablespoons of the butter over medium heat. Stir in olive oil. Add almonds; cook for 3 to 4 minutes or until almonds are lightly toasted, stirring frequently. Using a slotted spoon, remove almonds from pan; drain on paper towels. Set aside.

2. Add green beans, potatoes, shallots, garlic, and salt to butter mixture in pan. Toss to coat beans and potatoes. Add vegetable stock. Bring to a boil; reduce heat. Simmer for 10 to 15 minutes or until beans and potatoes are tender, tossing occasionally. Add the remaining 1 tablespoon butter, tossing to coat beans and potatoes. Sprinkle with pepper. Sprinkle with almonds.

SEE PHOTO, PAGE 47

CORN PUDDING

prep: 15 minutes / cook: 1¼ hours / serves 6

2	cups Alabama sweet corn kernels
	Salt
2	eggs, lightly beaten
2	tablespoons unsalted butter, melted
1	tablespoon sugar
2	cups milk

1. Preheat oven to 325°F. Lightly grease a 1½-quart baking dish; set aside. In a medium saucepan combine a small amount of water and corn. Season with salt. Bring to a boil; reduce heat. Simmer, covered, about 4 minutes or until corn is tender. Drain.

2. Stir eggs, butter, sugar, and 1 teaspoon salt into corn. In a small saucepan heat milk until hot but not boiling. Pour milk into corn mixture. Transfer corn mixture to prepared casserole.

3. Bake for 1¼ to 1½ hours or until the tip of a knife inserted near the center comes out clean.

CREAMED CAULIFLOWER WITH BLUE CHEESE

start to finish: 30 minutes / serves 6

1 tablespoon olive oil
1 medium onion, sliced
1 teaspoon chopped garlic
1 teaspoon chopped shallots
1 large head cauliflower, broken
   into florets
   Kosher salt
   Black pepper
¼ cup chicken stock
½ cup heavy cream
½ cup crumbled blue cheese
1 tablespoon unsalted butter

1. In a large stockpot heat olive oil over medium-high heat. Add onion, garlic, and shallots; sauté about 5 minutes or until onion is transparent and soft but not brown. Add cauliflower. Season to taste with salt and pepper. Add chicken stock; bring to a boil. Reduce heat to a simmer.

2. Add cream; simmer for 8 to 10 minutes or until cauliflower is tender. Stir in blue cheese until melted. Finish with butter.

SWEET CARROTS

start to finish: 15 minutes / serves 6

1¼ pounds baby carrots with tops,
   trimmed and peeled
1 tablespoon unsalted butter
1 tablespoon packed brown sugar
   Pinch ground nutmeg
1 tablespoon honey
1 tablespoon pineapple juice

1. In a steamer set over boiling water, steam the carrots for 4 to 8 minutes or just until tender; transfer to a bowl.

2. In a skillet melt butter over medium heat. Stir in brown sugar and nutmeg. Stir in honey and pineapple juice until smooth. Add carrots to skillet. Cook and stir over medium-low heat for 1 to 2 minutes or until carrots are evenly glazed and heated through.

CARROT SOUFFLÉ

prep: 25 minutes / bake: 1 hour / serves 6

Salt
1 pound carrots, peeled and cut into ¼-inch-thick slices
1 cup sugar
1 cup milk
½ cup (1 stick) unsalted butter, softened
3 eggs
3 tablespoons all-purpose flour
1 teaspoon baking powder
¼ teaspoon ground cinnamon
Powdered sugar (optional)

1. Preheat oven to 350°F. Lightly grease a 1-quart soufflé dish or casserole; set aside. In a saucepan bring water to a boil; add salt. Add carrots; return to boiling. Reduce heat; cover and simmer for 10 to 12 minutes or until carrots are tender. Drain. Place in a food processor or blender. Cover and process or blend until smooth.

2. Add sugar, milk, butter, eggs, flour, baking powder, ½ teaspoon salt, and the cinnamon to carrots in food processor or blender. Cover and process or blend until smooth. Pour into prepared soufflé dish.

3. Bake about 1 hour or until puffed and lightly golden. If desired, sprinkle with powdered sugar.

BAKED SUMMER SQUASH AND TOMATOES

start to finish: 25 minutes / serves 6

2 tablespoons olive oil
2 tablespoons diced shallots
2 tablespoons diced garlic
1 medium zucchini, cut into ¼-inch-thick slices
1 medium yellow squash, cut into ¼-inch-thick slices
1 large red bell pepper, seeded and diced into ½-inch pieces
1 16-ounce can plum tomatoes or one 14½-ounce can whole peeled tomatoes, drained and diced
1 teaspoon Italian seasoning
Pinch dried oregano
Kosher salt
Black pepper
2 tablespoons shredded Parmesan cheese

1. Preheat oven to 350°F. In a large oven-going skillet heat olive oil over medium heat; add shallots and garlic. Sauté until shallots are soft.

2. Add zucchini, yellow squash, bell pepper, tomatoes, Italian seasoning, and oregano. Season with salt and black pepper. Bake for 4 to 5 minutes or until squash is soft but not mushy. Spoon into a serving bowl; sprinkle with Parmesan cheese.

SWEET POTATO BREAD

prep: 20 minutes / cook: 25 minutes / bake: 1 hour / cool: 10 minutes / makes 2 loaves (30 slices)

12 ounces Alabama sweet potatoes, peeled and quartered
3½ cups sugar
1 cup cooking oil
4 eggs, lightly beaten
1 teaspoon vanilla extract
3½ cups all-purpose flour
1 teaspoon baking soda
1 teaspoon ground cinnamon
1 teaspoon ground nutmeg
1 teaspoon ground cloves
½ teaspoon salt
Citrus Butter

1. In large pot bring water to a boil; add sweet potatoes. Cover and simmer for 25 to 30 minutes or until tender; drain. Return to pot; using a potato masher, mash potatoes until smooth.

2. Preheat oven to 350°F. Grease bottom and ½ inch up sides of two 8×4×2-inch loaf pans; set aside. In a large bowl combine sweet potatoes, sugar, cooking oil, eggs, and vanilla extract. In another large bowl combine flour, baking soda, cinnamon, nutmeg, cloves, and salt. Add sweet potato mixture all at once to flour mixture. Stir just until moistened (batter should be lumpy). Spoon into prepared pans.

3. Bake about 1 hour or until a wooden toothpick inserted near centers comes out clean (if necessary to prevent overbrowning, cover loosely with foil the last 15 minutes of baking). Cool in pans on wire racks for 10 minutes. Remove from pans. Cool completely on wire racks. Serve with Citrus Butter.

CITRUS BUTTER: In a bowl combine ½ cup (1 stick) butter, softened; 1 tablespoon powdered sugar; and 1 teaspoon finely shredded orange or lemon zest.

G'S NOTE: FOR THE BEST TEXTURE, COOL THE LOAVES COMPLETELY, THEN WRAP IN PLASTIC WRAP AND STORE OVERNIGHT BEFORE SLICING.

TWICE-BAKED POTATOES

prep: 30 minutes / bake: 1 hour 25 minutes / serves 8

4 large baking potatoes
8 slices bacon
1 cup sour cream
1 cup shredded cheddar-Monterey Jack cheese
½ cup milk
¼ cup (½ stick) unsalted butter, softened
½ teaspoon salt
½ teaspoon black pepper
1 bunch fresh chives, chopped

1. Preheat oven to 350°F. Bake potatoes for 1 hour 10 minutes to 1 hour 20 minutes or until tender. Cool for 10 minutes.

2. Meanwhile, in a large skillet cook bacon until crisp. Drain on paper towels; crumble. Set aside.

3. Slice potatoes in half lengthwise; scoop out flesh (see photo below). Set skins aside. Place flesh in a large mixing bowl; stir in sour cream, ½ cup of the cheese, the milk, butter, salt, and pepper. Beat with an electric mixer on medium speed until potato mixture is well blended and creamy. Spoon mixture into potato skins.

4. Place potatoes on a baking sheet. Top with the remaining ½ cup cheese, the chives, and bacon. Bake about 15 minutes more or until heated through.

ROASTED POTATOES

prep: 20 minutes / roast: 20 minutes / serves 8

3   tablespoons olive oil
3   tablespoons minced garlic
2   tablespoons minced shallots
1   teaspoon G's Salt Seasoning
1   teaspoon fresh chopped
      rosemary
1   teaspoon crushed red pepper
2   pounds Yukon Gold potatoes,
      cut into eighths
½   cup (1 stick) unsalted
      butter, melted
1   bunch fresh chives,
      finely chopped
2   tablespoons chopped
      fresh parsley
    Salt
    Black pepper

1. Preheat oven to 475°F. In large bowl combine olive oil, garlic, shallots, Salt Seasoning, rosemary, and crushed red pepper. Add potatoes, tossing to coat. Arrange seasoned potatoes in a single layer in a baking pan. Roast for 20 to 30 minutes or until potatoes are golden around the edges, crisp, and tender when pierced with a fork.

2. Transfer potatoes to a large bowl; toss with melted butter, chives, and parsley. Season with salt and black pepper.

SEE PHOTO, PAGE 42

G'S NOTE:--

THESE POTATOES ARE GREAT ON THEIR OWN, OR YOU CAN SERVE THEM WITH A SIMPLE AÏOLI. TO MAKE THE AÏOLI, COMBINE 1 CUP MAYONNAISE; 3 TABLESPOONS LEMON JUICE; 3 CLOVES GARLIC, MINCED; AND A PINCH SALT. IF YOU LIKE, ADD SOME CHOPPED FRESH HERBS AND PAPRIKA.

PENNE RIGATE WITH CRISPY
PANCETTA, ONION, AND TOMATO SAUCE

start to finish: 25 minutes / serves 6

1   16-ounce package dried
     penne rigate pasta
1½ cups diced pancetta
1   white onion, diced
1   26-ounce jar tomato-base pasta
     sauce (any flavor)
     Pinch chopped fresh thyme
     Kosher salt
     Cracked black pepper

1. In a large pot bring water to a boil. Add penne rigate; cook according to package directions. Drain; return to hot pot. Keep warm.

2. Meanwhile, heat a medium sauté pan over medium heat. Add pancetta; sauté until pancetta is crispy. Drain pancetta, reserving about 2 tablespoons of the drippings in pan. Set pancetta aside. Add onion to sauté pan; sauté about 5 minutes or until onion is soft. Stir in pancetta and pasta sauce; heat through. Add penne rigate, tossing to coat. Stir in thyme. Season to taste with salt and pepper.

ANGEL HAIR PASTA WITH
TOMATOES AND SAUTÉED SHALLOTS

start to finish: 25 minutes / serves 8

     Kosher salt
1½ pounds dried angel hair pasta
1   tablespoon olive oil
1   cup peeled and diced plum
     tomatoes
½   cup sliced shallots
⅓   cup yellow grape or cherry
     tomatoes
⅓   cup red grape or cherry tomatoes
     Cracked white pepper
2   cups white wine
2   tablespoons unsalted butter

1. In a large saucepot bring water to a boil; add salt. Add pasta; cook according to package directions. Drain pasta; return to hot saucepot. Keep warm.

2. Meanwhile, in a medium sauté pan heat olive oil over medium heat. Add plum tomatoes, shallots, and grape tomatoes to hot oil. Season with salt and white pepper. Sauté for 6 to 8 minutes or until tomatoes are soft. Add cooking wine and butter; cook for 2 minutes more.

3. Add tomato mixture to pasta; toss until well mixed. Check seasoning.

RIGATONI WITH SWEET PEAS AND CRISPY PROSCIUTTO IN CREAM SAUCE

start to finish: 25 minutes / serves 8

1   16-ounce package dried rigatoni
     pasta
12 slices prosciutto
3   cups heavy cream
1½ cups fresh sweet peas
     Kosher salt
     Ground white pepper

1. Preheat oven to 400°F. In a large pot bring water to a boil. Add rigatoni; cook according to package directions. Drain; return to hot pot. Keep warm.

2. Meanwhile, arrange prosciutto on a baking sheet. Bake for 6 to 8 minutes or until fat turns golden and meat darkens slightly. Drain on paper towels (prosciutto will crisp more as it cools). Crumble prosciutto; set aside.

3. In a large sauté pan heat cream over medium heat for 5 to 8 minutes or until it thickens slightly. Stir in peas; heat through. Season with salt and white pepper. Add pasta to cream mixture, tossing to coat. Transfer to a serving platter; sprinkle with crumbled prosciutto.

G'S NOTE: ------------------------------------

GO AHEAD AND SUBSTITUTE CRISP-COOKED BACON FOR THE PROSCIUTTO, IF YOU LIKE.

MY LITTLE ONE'S FAVORITE LINGUINE WITH BUTTER AND PARMESAN CHEESE

start to finish: 15 minutes / serves 6

1   16-ounce package dried
     linguine pasta
¼   cup grated Parmesan cheese
3   tablespoons unsalted butter
     Kosher salt
     Ground white pepper

1. In a large pot bring water to a boil. Add linguine; cook according to package directions. Drain. Return linguine to hot pot. Add Parmesan cheese and butter, tossing to coat linguine. Season with salt and white pepper.

THREE-OLIVE FETA CHEESE SALAD

start to finish: 20 minutes / serves 6

½ cup kalamata olives
½ cup pitted Spanish olives
½ cup pitted black olives
½ cup crumbled feta cheese
¼ cup diced green bell pepper
¼ cup diced yellow bell pepper
3 tablespoons lemon juice
2 tablespoons olive oil
2 cloves garlic, thinly sliced
  Pinch crushed red pepper
18 Belgian endive leaves

1. In a large bowl combine olives, feta cheese, bell peppers, lemon juice, olive oil, garlic, and crushed red pepper.

2. Arrange three Belgian endive leaves, points out, on each of six salad plates. Spoon ½ cup of the olive mixture in the center of each plate, overlapping onto the edge of each endive leaf.

JALAPEÑO CHEESE GRITS

start to finish: 30 minutes / serves 8 to 10

3½ cups chicken stock
1¾ cups quick-cooking grits
½ cup (1 stick) unsalted butter
1 large green bell pepper, seeded and chopped
1 medium onion, chopped
2 red or green jalapeño chile peppers, seeded and diced*
2 cups shredded sharp cheddar cheese
2 cups shredded Monterey Jack cheese
  Black pepper
  Salt

1. In a medium saucepan bring chicken stock to a boil; stir in grits. Reduce heat. Simmer for 10 minutes. Cover; remove from heat.

2. In large skillet melt butter over medium heat; add bell pepper, onion, and jalapeño peppers. Sauté about 5 minutes or until vegetables are tender. Stir in grits, cheddar cheese, and Monterey Jack cheese. Season with salt and black pepper.

*NOTE: Because chile peppers contain volatile oils that can burn your skin and eyes, avoid direct contact with them as much as possible. When working with chile peppers, wear plastic or rubber gloves. If your bare hands do touch the peppers, wash your hands and nails well with soap and warm water.

THREE-CHEESE ANDOUILLE-AND-SPINACH- STUFFED TOMATOES

prep: 25 minutes / stand: 5 minutes / bake: 30 minutes / serves 8

2   10-ounce packages frozen
    chopped spinach
8   medium vine-ripened tomatoes
    Salt
1   cup diced cooked
    andouille sausage
1   cup fine dry bread crumbs
⅓   cup grated Parmesan cheese
⅓   cup shredded mozzarella cheese
⅓   cup shredded provolone cheese
2   eggs, lightly beaten
3   scallions, chopped
3   tablespoons unsalted
    butter, melted
½   teaspoon chopped fresh thyme
½   teaspoon G's Salt Seasoning
¼   teaspoon G's Garlic Salt
    Dash hot pepper sauce

1. Preheat oven to 325°F. Cook spinach according to package directions. Spoon spinach into a strainer; press with the back of a spoon to drain well (see photo below). Set spinach aside; discard liquid. Cut tops from tomatoes; remove pulp, leaving shells intact. Sprinkle insides of shells with salt. Invert on paper towels to drain; let stand for 5 minutes.

2. For filling, in a bowl combine spinach, andouille sausage, bread crumbs, Parmesan cheese, mozzarella cheese, provolone cheese, eggs, scallions, butter, thyme, Salt Seasoning, Garlic Salt, and hot pepper sauce.

3. Spoon filling into tomato shells. Arrange tomatoes in a baking pan. Bake for 30 minutes.

KICKED UP VEGETABLE MEDLEY

prep: 25 minutes / marinate: 30 minutes / cook: 10 minutes / serves 6

12　large fresh button
　　mushrooms, sliced
½　cup thickly sliced zucchini
½　cup sliced yellow squash
½　cup sliced red bell pepper
½　cup sliced yellow bell pepper
½　cup sliced red onion
12　cherry tomatoes
½　cup soy sauce
½　cup lemon juice
½　cup olive oil
2　teaspoons crushed red pepper
½　clove garlic, crushed
1　tablespoon olive oil
　　G's Salt Seasoning
　　Salt
　　Black pepper

1. In a large bowl combine mushrooms, zucchini, yellow squash, bell peppers, red onion, and cherry tomatoes. In a small bowl combine soy sauce, lemon juice, the ½ cup olive oil, the crushed red pepper, and garlic. Pour over vegetables, stirring to coat. Cover and marinate in the refrigerator for 30 minutes.

2. In a large sauté pan heat the 1 tablespoon olive oil over medium heat. Drain vegetables; discard marinade. Add vegetables to hot oil and sauté for 10 to 12 minutes or until tender. Season to taste with Salt Seasoning, salt, and black pepper.

GRILLED VEGETABLE SANDWICHES
WITH FRESH MOZZARELLA AND ARUGULA

prep: 25 minutes / cook: 5 minutes / makes 2 sandwiches

1 medium zucchini
1 medium eggplant, peeled
1 large red bell pepper, seeded and
   cut into 8 pieces
2 large portobello mushrooms,
   stems removed
1 medium red onion, cut into
   ¼-inch-thick slices
¼ cup olive oil
   Kosher salt
   Coarsely ground black pepper
2 focaccia rolls, split and toasted
¼ cup balsamic vinaigrette
   salad dressing
12 fresh arugula leaves
1 pound fresh mozzarella,
   cut into 8 slices

1. Cut zucchini and eggplant lengthwise into ¼-inch-thick slices; cut crosswise into 4-inch-long slices. Flatten bell pepper pieces. Brush mushrooms with a vegetable brush; wipe clean with a wet paper towel. In a large bowl combine zucchini, eggplant, bell pepper, mushrooms, and red onion. Drizzle with olive oil, tossing to coat. Season with salt and black pepper.

2. Heat a grill pan over medium-high heat. Place vegetables in grill pan; cook for 5 to 10 minutes, turning to brown evenly. Remove vegetables from grill pan as they become brown and cooked through. Set aside.

3. Drizzle cut sides of rolls with some of the salad dressing. Place roll bottoms, dressing sides up, on a flat surface. Divide vegetables between the roll bottoms. Place six arugula leaves on top of each. Top each with four slices of cheese. Add roll tops, dressing sides down.

BRIOCHE FRIES

start to finish: 15 minutes / serves 18

1 loaf brioche (about 16 ounces)
½ cup (1 stick) unsalted butter
1 teaspoon minced garlic

1. Cut bread into 3-inch-long bite-size strips. In a large skillet heat 2 tablespoons of the butter and ¼ teaspoon of the garlic over medium heat until melted. Add one-quarter of the bread strips; sauté until golden brown. Drain on paper towels. Repeat three more times with the remaining bread strips, butter, and garlic.

SEE PHOTO, PAGE 41

DON'T BE SCARED

Even if you don't know how to cook, you can make magic happen in the kitchen. I give you my easiest recipes—ones you can feel good about. Trust your boy. – G

I often run into people who love food and the whole idea of cooking but seem afraid to take on the challenge of making a meal themselves. They think cooking is much more difficult than it really is, and they just shut down. Don't be afraid of cooking a meal! The only rule you need to follow is this: Your house, your rules. Whatever you make, someone will eat. (And there's always a hungry neighbor.) Choose any of the easy-to-make favorites in this chapter, practice fixing it a few times, and before you know it, you've mastered your first great dish. Then when I see you on the street, you can tell me your story about your first meal and say to me, "G. Garvin, I'm not scared anymore."

SO TAKE THE FIRST STEP:
GET IN THE KITCHEN AND GET GOING.

MEAT LOVER'S MEAT LOAF

prep: 20 minutes / bake: 70 minutes / stand: 10 minutes / serves 8

8   ounces ground beef
8   ounces ground veal
8   ounces ground pork
1   cup fresh bread crumbs
½   cup chopped green bell pepper
2   eggs, lightly beaten
⅓   cup minced fresh parsley
1   tablespoon minced garlic
1   tablespoon chopped shallots
1   teaspoon garlic powder
    G's Salt Seasoning
    Salt
    Black pepper
    Bottled barbecue sauce

1. Preheat oven to 350°F. In a bowl combine meats, bread crumbs, bell pepper, eggs, parsley, minced garlic, shallots, and garlic powder. Season with Salt Seasoning, salt, and black pepper, mixing well. Lightly pat mixture into an 8×4×2-inch loaf pan.

2. Bake for 1 to 1¼ hours or until done (160°F).* Spoon off fat. Spoon barbecue sauce over meat. Bake for 10 minutes more. Let stand for 10 minutes before serving.

*NOTE: The internal color of a meat loaf is not a reliable doneness indicator. A beef, veal, or pork loaf cooked to 160°F is safe, regardless of color. To measure the doneness of a meat loaf, insert an instant-read thermometer into the center of the loaf.

TOASTED MEATBALL SANDWICHES
WITH PROVOLONE CHEESE AND SAUTÉED PEPPERS

start to finish: 30 minutes / makes 4 sandwiches

2 tablespoons olive oil

1 red bell pepper, seeded and cut into strips

1 green bell pepper, seeded and cut into strips

2 teaspoons minced garlic

G's Meatballs

2¼ cups tomato-base pasta sauce (any flavor)

Kosher salt

Black pepper

2 tablespoons unsalted butter

4 8-inch hoagie rolls, split

12 slices fresh provolone cheese

1. Preheat oven to 350°F. In a large sauté pan heat olive oil over medium heat. Add bell peppers and garlic; sauté about 4 minutes or until peppers are tender. Stir in G's Meatballs and pasta sauce; season with salt and black pepper. Cook on low heat for 4 minutes more while you prepare the hoagie rolls.

2. Spread butter on the inside of each hoagie roll. Place rolls on a baking sheet. Bake for 5 to 7 minutes. Remove rolls from oven.

3. Fill each roll with three slices provolone cheese and five meatballs. Spoon some of the bell pepper mixture over meatballs in each roll.

G'S MEATBALLS: Preheat oven to 350°F. In a large bowl combine 8 ounces ground beef, 8 ounces veal, 1 egg, 2 teaspoons bread crumbs, 2 teaspoons chopped fresh basil, 2 teaspoons olive oil, 1 teaspoon chopped garlic, 1 teaspoon chopped shallot, ½ teaspoon salt, and ½ teaspoon black pepper. Mix well; roll meat mixture into 20 meatballs. In a sauté pan, heat 2 tablespoons olive oil over medium-high heat. Sauté meatballs in pan about 5 minutes or until brown. Remove meatballs from pan and place in a shallow baking pan. Bake for 5 to 7 minutes or until firm and cooked through. Drain meatballs on paper towels.

G'S GOTTA-BE-QUICK TIP: ----------------
IF YOU'RE PRESSED FOR TIME, PURCHASE A PACKAGE OF FROZEN ITALIAN-STYLE MEATBALLS. THAW 20 OF THEM FOR TOASTED MEATBALL SANDWICHES WITH PROVOLONE CHEESE AND SAUTÉED PEPPERS.

HERB-CRUSTED BEEF TENDERLOIN
WITH YUKON GOLD POTATOES AND CARROTS

prep: 20 minutes / roast: 35 minutes / stand: 15 minutes / serves 8

¼ cup chopped fresh rosemary

¼ cup chopped fresh thyme

¼ cup chopped fresh
     flat-leaf parsley

¼ cup minced garlic

2 tablespoons diced shallots

1 2-pound whole beef tenderloin

¼ teaspoon G's Salt Seasoning

¼ teaspoon G's Garlic Salt
     Kosher salt

4½ teaspoons cracked black pepper

2 tablespoons olive oil

8 ounces Yukon Gold potatoes,
     cut in 2-inch pieces

3 large carrots, cut in 2-inch pieces

1. Preheat oven to 425°F. In a bowl combine rosemary, thyme, parsley, garlic, and shallots; set aside. Season meat on all sides with Salt Seasoning, Garlic Salt, salt, and pepper. Press herb mixture onto meat.

2. In a roasting pan heat olive oil; add meat. Sear meat on all sides until brown. Remove pan from heat. Remove meat from pan. Drain off fat. Place a rack in the pan; position meat on the rack. Arrange potatoes and carrots around meat.

3. Roast meat for 35 to 40 minutes or until done (135° for medium-rare or 150°F for medium). Remove from oven; cover with foil. Let stand for 15 minutes.

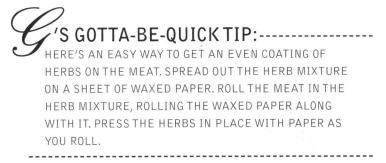

G'S GOTTA-BE-QUICK TIP:

HERE'S AN EASY WAY TO GET AN EVEN COATING OF HERBS ON THE MEAT. SPREAD OUT THE HERB MIXTURE ON A SHEET OF WAXED PAPER. ROLL THE MEAT IN THE HERB MIXTURE, ROLLING THE WAXED PAPER ALONG WITH IT. PRESS THE HERBS IN PLACE WITH PAPER AS YOU ROLL.

OLD-SCHOOL PORK CHOP SANDWICHES

prep: 10 minutes / cook: 8 minutes / makes 4 sandwiches

4   boneless pork loin or rib chops
    cut ¾ to 1 inch thick (about
    8 ounces each)
    G's Garlic Salt
    G's Salt Seasoning
2   cups all-purpose flour
2   tablespoons canola oil
8   thick slices wheat bread
3   tablespoons ketchup

1. Season chops with Garlic Salt and Salt Seasoning. Coat chops on both sides with flour, shaking off excess.

2. In a large sauté pan heat canola oil over medium heat. Add chops; cook 8 to 12 minutes or until done (160°F), turning once.

3. Top each of four of the bread slices with a chop; spread each with some of the ketchup. Top each with one of the remaining bread slices.

GRILLED SWISS CHEESE SANDWICHES
WITH SMOKED TURKEY AND TOMATO

prep: 10 minutes / cook: 4 minutes / makes 2 sandwiches

4   slices potato bread
8   slices Swiss cheese
8   ounces thinly sliced smoked
    turkey
1   teaspoon granulated garlic
1   vine-ripened tomato, thinly sliced
1   tablespoon unsalted butter

1. Top each of two of the bread slices with four of the Swiss cheese slices. Divide turkey between the two stacks. Sprinkle each stack with granulated garlic; divide tomato slices between the stacks. Add one of the remaining bread slices to each stack.

2. In a large sauté pan melt butter over medium heat; add sandwiches. Cook for 4 to 6 minutes or until cheese is melted and sandwiches are golden brown, turning once.

G'S NOTE: --

MAKE A MEAL BY SERVING THESE HEARTY
SANDWICHES WITH YOUR FAVORITE CHIPS AND
FRESH GRAPES.

BRAISED VEAL CHOPS WITH BUTTERED GREEN BEANS

prep: 15 minutes / cook: 23 minutes / serves 6

Kosher salt
8 ounces French green beans
    (haricots verts)
1 cup diced shallots
    Cracked white pepper
6 8-ounce veal chops
6 tablespoons olive oil
2 Spanish onions, sliced
8 sprigs fresh rosemary
1 cup white wine
1 cup chicken stock
¾ cup (1½ sticks) unsalted butter

1. In a large saucepan bring water to a boil; add salt. Add green beans; cook for 10 to 15 minutes or until crisp-tender. Drain beans; stir shallots into beans. Season to taste with salt and white pepper; set aside.

2. Meanwhile, season the veal chops on both sides with salt and white pepper. In an extra-large skillet heat olive oil over medium heat. Sear the chops on the first side for 3 minutes; turn chops. Add onions and rosemary. Stir in wine and chicken stock. Bring to a boil; reduce heat. Simmer for 2 minutes. Add butter and simmer about 15 minutes or until done (160°F).

3. To serve, arrange chops around the edge of a large platter. Place beans in the center of chops. Pour wine mixture from skillet over chops.

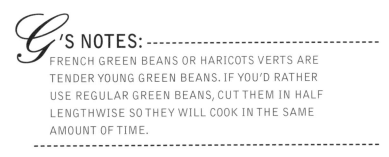

𝒢'S NOTES: ------------------------------------
FRENCH GREEN BEANS OR HARICOTS VERTS ARE
TENDER YOUNG GREEN BEANS. IF YOU'D RATHER
USE REGULAR GREEN BEANS, CUT THEM IN HALF
LENGTHWISE SO THEY WILL COOK IN THE SAME
AMOUNT OF TIME.

CRISPY OVEN-BAKED FISH

prep: 15 minutes / cook: 4 minutes per ½-inch thickness of fish / serves 6

1 cup cornflakes
¼ cup grated Parmesan cheese
¼ teaspoon dried thyme
1 egg, lightly beaten
¼ cup milk
2 pounds fresh fish fillets
   (cod, tilapia, red snapper,
   whitefish, or whiting)
   G's Salt Seasoning
   Salt
   Black pepper
⅓ cup unsalted butter, melted
   Chopped fresh parsley
   Lemon wedges

1. Heat oven to 450°F. Grease a baking dish; set aside. Place cornflakes in a resealable plastic bag. Using a rolling pin, crush cornflakes to form fine crumbs. In a shallow bowl combine cornflake crumbs, Parmesan cheese, and thyme. In another shallow bowl combine egg and milk.

2. Rinse fish; pat dry with paper towels. Measure thickness of fish. Season fish with Salt Seasoning, salt, and pepper. Dip fish in egg mixture and roll in crumb mixture. Place fish in prepared baking dish. Drizzle butter over fish. Sprinkle any remaining crumb mixture on top of fish. Bake for 4 to 6 minutes per ½-inch thickness of fish or until done.

3. Sprinkle fish with parsley. Serve with lemon wedges.

SWORDFISH WITH GREEN BEANS AND CHUNKY GUACAMOLE

start to finish: 35 minutes / serves 4

1 pound fresh green beans
   Kosher salt
4 6-ounce pieces skinless fresh
   swordfish, cut 1 inch thick
   Cracked white pepper
2 tablespoons olive oil
1 shallot, diced
   Chunky Guacamole

1. In a saucepan bring enough water to cover beans to a boil; add salt. Add green beans; cook for 10 to 15 minutes or until beans are tender. Drain beans; set aside.

2. Rinse fish; pat dry with paper towels. Measure thickness of fish. Season fish with salt and white pepper. In a sauté pan heat 1 tablespoon of the olive oil. Add fish; cook for 4 to 6 minutes per ½-inch thickness of fish or until done, turning once.

3. In another sauté pan heat remaining 1 tablespoon olive oil. Sauté green beans and shallot until shallot is tender.

4. To serve, place beans in the center of a platter. Arrange fish pieces around the edge of the platter. Top each fish piece with some of the Chunky Guacamole.

CHUNKY GUACAMOLE: In a bowl combine 3 Hass avocados, peeled, pitted, and diced; 2 small plum tomatoes, diced; ¼ of a small onion, diced; 1 bunch fresh cilantro, coarsely chopped; and 3 tablespoons lemon juice. Season to taste with Kosher salt and cracked white pepper.

BEGINNER'S SALMON

prep: 20 minutes / chill: 1 hour / grill: 4 minutes per ½-inch thickness of fish / serves 6

1 cup fresh basil leaves

6 tablespoons unsalted butter, softened

1 tablespoon chopped shallots

1 tablespoon minced garlic

1 tablespoon lemon juice

1 teaspoon chopped fresh rosemary

Salt

Black pepper

6 6-ounce fresh salmon steaks

1. For herb butter, in a food processor or blender combine basil, butter, shallots, garlic, lemon juice, and rosemary. Cover and process or blend until smooth. Season to taste with salt and pepper. Chill mixture in the refrigerator until firm enough to shape. Spoon butter mixture onto waxed paper; form into a log 1 inch in diameter (see photos below). Wrap log in plastic wrap. Chill in the refrigerator about 1 hour or until firm.

2. Rinse fish; pat dry with paper towels. Measure thickness of fish. Season fish with salt and pepper. Place fish on the greased rack of an uncovered grill directly over medium coals. Grill for 4 to 6 minutes per ½-inch thickness of fish or until done.

3. To serve, slice herb butter into six portions. Top each fish steak with a portion of the herb butter.

SUPER SIMPLE SCALLOPS

start to finish: 20 minutes / serves 4

1	pound large fresh sea scallops
2	tablespoons olive oil
2	tablespoons finely chopped fresh flat-leaf parsley
2	tablespoons finely chopped garlic
2	tablespoons chopped shallots
¼	cup chicken stock
½	teaspoon cornstarch
	Salt
	Cayenne pepper
	Hot cooked basmati rice

1. Rinse scallops; pat dry with paper towels. In a large skillet heat olive oil over medium heat. Add scallops, parsley, garlic, and shallots. Sauté for 2 to 3 minutes or until scallops are opaque. Using a slotted spoon, remove scallops from skillet.

2. In a small bowl stir together chicken stock and cornstarch. Stir into mixture in skillet: bring to a boil. Reduce heat; simmer for 2 to 3 minutes or until thickened and bubbly, stirring frequently. Return scallops to skillet. Season with salt and cayenne pepper.

3. To serve, spoon scallop mixture over hot cooked rice.

SUPER SIMPLE HONEY-GLAZED ARCTIC CHAR

start to finish: 25 minutes / serves 4

4	8-ounce pieces skinless fresh arctic char fillet or skinless fresh salmon fillets
	G's Salt Seasoning
2	tablespoons olive oil
1	tablespoon chopped garlic
1	tablespoon chopped shallots
2	tablespoons honey

1. Preheat broiler. Rinse fish; pat dry with paper towels. Measure thickness of fish. Season fish with Salt Seasoning; set aside. In a broilerproof sauté pan heat olive oil over medium heat. Add garlic and shallots; sauté until shallots are soft.

2. Add fish to pan. Cook for 4 to 6 minutes per ½-inch thickness of fish or until done, turning once.

3. Drizzle honey over fish. Broil 4 to 5 inches from heat for 1 to 2 minutes or until fish is lightly brown.

G'S NOTE: --------------------------------------

ARCTIC CHAR IS A PINK-FLESHED FISH THAT TASTES
LIKE A BLEND OF SALMON AND TROUT.

SEARED SEA SCALLOPS WITH CRISPY PROSCIUTTO AND GARLIC MASHED POTATOES

prep: 10 minutes / cook: 10 minutes / serves 6

2	pounds fresh sea scallops
	Kosher salt
	Cracked white pepper
½	cup olive oil
10	slices prosciutto
1	cup chicken stock
½	cup (1 stick) butter
	Garlic mashed potatoes
	(your favorite recipe)

1. Preheat oven to 350°F. Rinse scallops; pat dry with paper towels. Season with salt and pepper. In a large sauté pan heat olive oil over medium-high heat. Add scallops to hot oil; sear for 4 minutes or until scallops are white and firm, turning once halfway through cooking time. Remove from pan; keep warm.

2. Place prosciutto on a baking sheet. Bake for 4 to 5 minutes or until crispy. Remove from oven. Cut prosciutto on the bias into bite-size pieces; set aside.

3. Add chicken stock and butter to sauté pan; simmer over low heat for 2 minutes or until butter melts. Meanwhile, place some of the mashed potatoes in the center of each of six dinner plates. Divide the scallops among the plates, placing them around the potatoes in a uniform pattern. Place prosciutto in the center of the potatoes. Pour the stock mixture over scallops.

G'S GOTTA-BE-QUICK TIP: ------------------
IT'S A GOOD IDEA TO HAVE THE MASHED POTATOES ALREADY DONE BECAUSE THE SCALLOPS COOK PRETTY QUICKLY. TO MAKE GARLIC MASHED POTATOES, PREPARE YOUR FAVORITE MASHED POTATOES RECIPE, EXCEPT ADD 4 PEELED CLOVES OF GARLIC TO THE WATER WHILE COOKING THE POTATOES AND MASH THEM WITH THE POTATOES. ALSO SUBSTITUTE OLIVE OIL FOR THE BUTTER IN THE RECIPE.

A NEW TWIST ON OLD-FASHIONED GRILLED CHEESE

prep: 10 minutes / cook: 4 minutes / makes 2 sandwiches

4	slices prosciutto
8	slices Gruyère cheese
4	slices egg bread
6	pieces oil-packed sun-dried tomatoes, drained
2	tablespoons unsalted butter

1. Heat a large skillet over medium heat. Add prosciutto; cook until prosciutto is crispy. Drain prosciutto on paper towels; set aside.
2. Place two slices of the Gruyère cheese on each of two of the bread slices. Divide prosciutto and tomatoes between the stacks. Top each with two more slices of the Gruyère cheese and another bread slice. Press sandwiches together firmly.
3. Wipe out skillet with paper towels. Melt butter in skillet over medium heat. Add sandwiches; cook for 4 to 6 minutes or until cheese is melted and sandwiches are golden, turning once.

G'S NOTE:

PROSCIUTTO, THE MUCH LOVED HAM FROM PARMA, HAS A SLIGHTLY SWEET FLAVOR DEVELOPED THROUGH A LONG CURING PROCESS OF AT LEAST NINE MONTHS. IT'S DEFINITELY WORTH SEEKING OUT FROM A LOCAL ITALIAN DELI FOR ITS DEEP, RICH FLAVOR. YOU CAN ALSO TOSS CRISP-COOKED PROSCIUTTO INTO SALADS AND PASTAS.

SUPER SIMPLE CHEESY-SPINACH QUESADILLAS

prep: 15 minutes / broil: 1 minute / serves 2

4   12-inch whole wheat flour tortillas
1   cup shredded cheddar cheese
1   cup shredded Monterey
     Jack cheese
2   cups baby spinach
½   cup chopped scallions
⅛   teaspoon freshly ground
     black pepper
     Crushed red pepper (optional)
     Sour cream
     Mild or medium salsa

1. Preheat broiler. Place two of the tortillas on a baking sheet. Sprinkle ¼ cup of the cheddar cheese and ¼ cup of the Monterey Jack cheese over each tortilla. Divide spinach leaves and scallions between tortillas. Sprinkle each with ¼ cup of the cheddar cheese and ¼ cup of the Monterey Jack cheese. Sprinkle each with some of the black pepper and, if desired, crushed red pepper. Top each stack with one of the remaining tortillas.

2. Broil 4 to 5 inches from heat for 1 to 1½ minutes or until tortillas are lightly toasted and cheese is melted. Serve with sour cream and salsa.

G'S NOTE:--
FOR EXTRA SPINACH FLAVOR AND A FUN COLOR, USE
SPINACH-FLAVOR FLOUR TORTILLAS.

DOUBLE-DOWN CORN CHOWDER

prep: 20 minutes / cook: 10 minutes / serves 6

4   slices bacon
1   onion, chopped
2   shallots, minced
2   cloves garlic, minced
2   cups frozen hash brown
    potatoes, thawed
1   14-ounce can cream-style corn
1   14-ounce can condensed
    chicken broth
1   cup water
1   teaspoon crushed red pepper
    Chopped fresh parsley

1. In a large saucepan cook bacon until crisp. Remove bacon from saucepan, reserving drippings in saucepan. Drain bacon on paper towels; crumble.

2. Add onion, shallots, and garlic to drippings in saucepan; cook until soft. Stir in hash brown potatoes, corn, chicken broth, the water, and crushed red pepper. Bring to a boil; reduce heat. Simmer for 10 to 15 minutes or until desired consistency. Stir in bacon.

3. To serve, ladle into six soup bowls and sprinkle each serving with parsley.

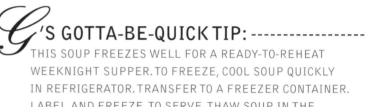

G'S GOTTA-BE-QUICK TIP: -----------------

THIS SOUP FREEZES WELL FOR A READY-TO-REHEAT WEEKNIGHT SUPPER. TO FREEZE, COOL SOUP QUICKLY IN REFRIGERATOR. TRANSFER TO A FREEZER CONTAINER. LABEL AND FREEZE. TO SERVE, THAW SOUP IN THE REFRIGERATOR. TRANSFER TO A SAUCEPAN. STIR IN ¼ CUP WATER. COOK AND STIR UNTIL BUBBLY. LADLE INTO SOUP BOWLS AND SPRINKLE WITH PARSLEY.

EGG SALAD PITA POCKETS

prep: 15 minutes / stand: 15 minutes / serves 4

6 extra-large eggs
2 tablespoons mayonnaise
1 tablespoon sweet pickle relish
1 teaspoon Dijon mustard
   Kosher salt
   Black pepper
2 pita bread rounds, halved
4 leaf lettuce leaves

1. Place eggs in a saucepan; add enough water to cover eggs by at least 1 inch. Bring to a boil over high heat. Remove pan from heat. Cover; let stand for 15 minutes. Drain; run cold water over eggs or place in ice water until cool enough to handle. Drain; peel and chop eggs. Place in a medium bowl.

2. Fold in mayonnaise, sweet pickle relish, and Dijon mustard. Season with salt and pepper.

3. Line each pita bread half with a lettuce leaf. Divide egg mixture among pita bread halves.

BANANA PANCAKES

start to finish: 20 minutes / makes 10 pancakes

$1\frac{1}{2}$ cups pancake mix
1 medium banana, mashed
1 teaspoon vanilla extract
   Pinch ground cinnamon
   Unsalted butter
   Maple syrup

1. In a large bowl prepare pancake mix according to package directions. Fold in banana, vanilla extract, and cinnamon.

2. For each pancake, pour about ¼ cup of the batter onto a hot lightly greased griddle or heavy skillet, spreading batter if necessary. Cook over medium heat for 2 to 4 minutes or until pancake is golden brown, turning to second side when pancake has a bubbly surface and edge is slightly dry. Serve with butter and maple syrup.

FIRE UP THE *G*RILL

Everything tastes better outdoors. So invite a few friends and fire up the grill. Bring out some salads, veggies, and drinks. It doesn't get any better than this! – G

BBQ season—it's time for everybody to bring his or her best game to the grill. Your uncle thinks he's got the best BBQ sauce. The brother-in-law says he's got the best baby backs. Auntie has the market cornered with the coleslaw. And the grown-up kids don't have enough experience to even stand next to the old vets! One of the things I love about BBQ season is that it gets you out of the house and away from the whole restaurant scene, so you can enjoy the day lounging around the pool, hanging in the park, or just kicking it in the backyard—playing cards or dominos and talking ish.

IT'S TIME TO FIRE UP THE GRILL . . .
SO WHO'S GOT GAME?

BACKYARD BBQ BEEF RIBS

prep: 10 minutes / grill: 1½ hours / serves 4

4 pounds beef back ribs, cut
    into serving-size portions
    G's Salt Seasoning
1½ cups cherry cola soft drink
1 cup ketchup
1 medium onion, finely chopped
¼ cup vinegar
¼ cup Worcestershire sauce
6 cloves garlic, finely chopped
2 teaspoons chili powder
2 teaspoons paprika
    Salt
    Black pepper

1. Season ribs with Salt Seasoning. Place medium-hot coals around a drip pan. Test for medium heat above the pan. Place ribs, bone sides down, on the grill rack over drip pan. Cover; grill for 1 hour.

2. Meanwhile, for sauce, in a saucepan combine cherry cola, ketchup, onion, vinegar, Worcestershire sauce, garlic, chili powder, and paprika. Season to taste with Salt Seasoning, salt, and pepper. Bring to a boil; reduce heat. Simmer for 10 to 15 minutes or until desired consistency.

3. Brush ribs on both sides with some of the sauce. Grill about 30 minutes more or until ribs are tender, basting with sauce and turning often. Serve with remaining sauce.

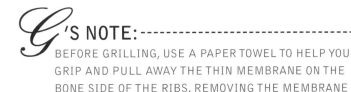

G's NOTE: BEFORE GRILLING, USE A PAPER TOWEL TO HELP YOU GRIP AND PULL AWAY THE THIN MEMBRANE ON THE BONE SIDE OF THE RIBS. REMOVING THE MEMBRANE WILL MAKE THE RIBS EASIER TO EAT.

GRILLED T-BONE STEAKS
WITH PARSLEY-AND-GARLIC SAUCE

prep: 15 minutes / grill: 10 minutes / serves 4

4 beef T-bone steaks, cut 2 to
   3 inches thick (about
   12 ounces each)
   Parsley-and-Garlic Sauce

1. Place steaks on the rack of an uncovered grill directly over medium coals. Grill to desired doneness. Allow 10 to 13 minutes for medium-rare (145°F) or 12 to 15 minutes for medium (160°F). Serve steaks with Parsley-and-Garlic Sauce.

PARSLEY-AND-GARLIC SAUCE: In a saucepan bring water to a boil; add 1½ bunches fresh flat-leaf parsley. Cook for 2 minutes. Using a slotted spoon, quickly remove parsley from water; cool in ice water. Drain on paper towels. In a food processor combine parsley; ½ cup minced garlic; ½ of a bunch fresh rosemary, stems removed; ½ of a bunch fresh thyme, stems removed; and ½ cup olive oil. Cover and process until smooth. With the food processor running, alternately add 4 ounces fresh baby spinach and 1 cup olive oil, a little at a time through the feed tube, processing until all is combined. Stir in 1 teaspoon kosher salt, 1 teaspoon fresh cracked black pepper, and ½ teaspoon crushed red pepper.

SEE PHOTO, PAGE 42

G'S GOTTA-BE-QUICK TIP:-----------------
THE PARSLEY-AND-GARLIC SAUCE CAN BE MADE AND
REFRIGERATED UP TO A WEEK BEFORE USING. FOR
A GREAT MEAL, SERVE THE STEAK WITH ROASTED
HERBED POTATOES.

GUINNESS®-MARINATED RIBEYES

prep: 20 minutes / marinate: 30 minutes / grill: 10 minutes / serves 4

1 small onion, chopped
8 garlic cloves, chopped
4 teaspoons chopped shallots
1 tablespoon finely chopped
   fresh tarragon
1 tablespoon finely chopped
   fresh parsley
1 12-ounce can Guinness® stout,
   at room temperature
¼ cup soy sauce
2 tablespoons packed brown sugar
2 tablespoons browning sauce
   (such as Kitchen Bouquet®)
1 teaspoon Dijon mustard
1 teaspoon Worcestershire sauce
   Salt
   Coarsely ground black pepper
4 beef ribeye steaks, cut 1 inch
   thick (about 12 ounces each)

1. For marinade, in a bowl combine onion, garlic, shallots, tarragon, and parsley. In another bowl combine stout, soy sauce, brown sugar, browning sauce, Dijon mustard, and Worcestershire sauce. Stir into onion mixture; season with salt and pepper.

2. Place steaks in a resealable plastic bag set in a shallow bowl. Pour marinade over meat. Seal bag. Marinate in the refrigerator for 30 minutes, turning occasionally.

3. Drain meat, reserving marinade. Place meat on the rack of an uncovered grill directly over medium coals. Grill to desired doneness. Allow 10 to 12 minutes for medium-rare (145°F) or 12 to 15 minutes for medium (160°F), turning once.

4. Meanwhile, in a small saucepan bring the reserved marinade to a boil;* reduce heat. Simmer about 5 minutes or until slightly thickened. Serve with meat.

*NOTE: Before serving the marinade, be sure to bring it to a full boil and simmer it for 5 minutes in order to destroy any bacteria from the raw meat.

GRILLED WHOLE SKIRT STEAK WITH BBQ SEASONING

prep: 5 minutes / grill: 14 minutes / stand: 5 minutes / serves 10 to 12

1	3-pound beef skirt steak
1	tablespoon olive oil
¼	cup G's BBQ Spice Rub

1. Rub both sides of meat with olive oil. Sprinkle both sides with BBQ Spice Rub, working it in with your fingers.

2. Place meat on the rack of an uncovered grill directly over medium coals. Grill meat for 14 to 18 minutes or until medium doneness (160°F), turning once. Remove from grill; let stand for 5 minutes to cool slightly. Thinly slice meat diagonally across the grain.

G'S NOTE: --
I LIKE SERVING THIS ZESTY STEAK WITH GARLIC-ROASTED
POTATOES AND SOME FRESH VEGGIE PIECES GRILLED
ALONGSIDE THE MEAT.

GRILLED BOURBON-MARINATED SKIRT STEAK DELUXE

prep: 20 minutes / marinate: 30 minutes to 1 hour / grill: 8 minutes / stand: 5 minutes / serves 4

1 cup soy sauce
½ cup finely chopped red onion
¼ cup packed brown sugar
¼ cup Worcestershire sauce
¼ cup bourbon
2 tablespoons chopped shallots
2 tablespoons chopped garlic
1 tablespoon olive oil
1 teaspoon dry mustard
  Kosher salt
  Coarsely ground black pepper
2 8-ounce pieces beef skirt steak
½ cup (1 stick) unsalted butter,
  softened
1 teaspoon dried parsley flakes
4 6-inch Cuban rolls or
  4 kaiser rolls, split
2 large heirloom tomatoes, sliced
16 slices mozzarella cheese

1. For marinade, in a bowl whisk together soy sauce, red onion, brown sugar, Worcestershire sauce, bourbon, shallots, 1 tablespoon of the garlic, the olive oil, mustard, a pinch of salt, and a pinch of pepper. Place meat in a resealable plastic bag set in a shallow dish. Pour marinade over meat; seal bag. Marinate in the refrigerator for at least 30 minutes or up to 1 hour, turning occasionally.

2. Meanwhile, preheat broiler. In a small bowl whip together butter, the remaining 1 tablespoon garlic, the parsley, a pinch of salt, and a pinch of pepper. Spread butter mixture on cut sides of rolls. Place rolls, buttered sides up, on a baking sheet. Broil for 1 to 2 minutes or until edges of the rolls start to brown. Remove from broiler; set aside.

3. Remove meat from marinade; discard marinade. Place meat on the rack of an uncovered grill directly over medium coals. Grill about 8 minutes or until medium doneness (160°F), turning once. Remove from grill; let stand for 5 minutes to cool slightly. Thinly slice meat diagonally across the grain.

4. Divide meat slices among roll bottoms. Top each sandwich with some of the tomato slices. Add four slices of mozzarella cheese to each sandwich. Return to broiler; broil for 1 to 2 minutes or until cheese is melted and bubbly. Top sandwiches with roll tops. Cut in half and serve.

G'S NOTE: --
IF YOUR SUPERMARKET DOESN'T ROUTINELY CARRY
SKIRT STEAK, LOOK FOR IT AT AN HISPANIC FOOD
MARKET OR ASK YOUR BUTCHER TO ORDER SKIRT STEAK
FOR YOU.

ZESTY BURGERS WITH HORSERADISH AND SEASONINGS

prep: 15 minutes / grill: 10 minutes / serves 4 to 6

1   to 1½ pounds lean ground beef
¼   cup chopped shallots
¼   cup chopped garlic
3   tablespoons barbecue sauce
2   tablespoons finely chopped green
       bell pepper
1   tablespoon prepared horseradish
2   teaspoons Dijon mustard
1   teaspoon salt
       Dash black pepper
4   to 6 potato bread hamburger buns
       Toppings (lettuce, tomato, onions,
       pickles, mustard, mayonnaise,
       and/or ketchup)

1. In a large bowl combine ground beef, shallots, garlic, barbecue sauce, bell pepper, horseradish, Dijon mustard, salt, and black pepper. Shape into four to six patties, each about ½ inch thick.

2. Place patties on the rack of an uncovered grill directly over medium coals. Grill for 10 to 13 minutes or until done (160°F),* turning once.

3. Serve burgers on hamburger buns with desired toppings.

*NOTE: The internal color of a burger is not a reliable doneness indicator. A beef patty cooked to 160°F is safe, regardless of color. To measure the doneness of a patty, insert an instant-read thermometer through the side of the patty to a depth of 2 to 3 inches.

GRILLED FILET BURGERS

prep: 15 minutes / grill: 14 minutes / serves 4

2   pounds ground beef tenderloin
1   large egg, lightly beaten
2   tablespoons diced shallots
1   tablespoon steak sauce
       (such as A.1.®)
1   teaspoon minced garlic
1   teaspoon onion powder
1   teaspoon G's Salt Seasoning
½   teaspoon kosher salt
4   sourdough hamburger
       buns, split
       Dijon mustard
       Crumbled Roquefort cheese

1. In a medium bowl combine ground beef, egg, shallots, steak sauce, garlic, onion powder, Salt Seasoning, and salt. Shape into four ¾-inch-thick patties.

2. Place patties on the grill rack of an uncovered grill directly over medium coals. Grill for 14 to 18 minutes or until done (160°F; see note above), turning once.

3. To serve, spread cut sides of hamburger buns with Dijon mustard. Place patties on bun bottoms. Top each with Roquefort cheese; add bun tops.

G'S NOTES: -----------------------------------

BEEF TENDERLOIN IS THE CUT OF MEAT USED FOR FILET MIGNON. HAVE YOUR BUTCHER GRIND SOME FOR YOU TO MAKE THESE SUCCULENT BURGERS OR FINELY CHOP THE MEAT IN A FOOD PROCESSOR.

BBQ SPICE-RUBBED PORK LOIN AND ZESTY SALSA

prep: 20 minutes / marinate: 15 minutes / grill: 6 minutes / serves 8 to 12

3 **pounds boneless pork loin**
   G's Salt Seasoning
   G's BBQ Spice Rub
¼ **cup olive oil**
   Zesty Salsa

1. Trim fat from pork; cut into ½-inch-thick slices. Season slices on both sides with Salt Seasoning and BBQ Spice Rub. Brush slices on both sides with olive oil; rub seasonings and oil into meat with your fingers. Marinate in the refrigerator for 15 minutes.

2. Place meat slices on the rack of an uncovered grill directly over medium coals. Grill for 6 to 8 minutes or until done (160°F), turning once. Serve meat slices with Zesty Salsa.

ZESTY SALSA: In a bowl combine 3 large tomatoes, diced; 1 medium yellow bell pepper, seeded and diced; 1 medium red bell pepper, seeded and diced; ½ of a small onion, diced; ¼ cup chopped scallions; 2 fresh jalapeño chile peppers, chopped;* 6 cloves garlic, minced; 2 tablespoons apple cider vinegar; 1 tablespoon chopped fresh cilantro; and 1 teaspoon chili powder. Season with kosher salt and black pepper.

*NOTE: Because chile peppers contain volatile oils that can burn your skin and eyes, avoid direct contact with them as much as possible. When working with chile peppers, wear plastic or rubber gloves. If your bare hands do touch the peppers, wash your hands and nails well with soap and warm water.

SEE PHOTO, PAGE 47

G'S GOTTA-BE-QUICK TIP:-----------------
FOR AN EASY AND FLAVORFUL SIDE, TRY STEAMED
WHOLE GREEN BEANS.

BARBECUED PORK TENDERLOIN WITH GRILLED ONIONS

prep: 15 minutes / marinate: 30 minutes / grill: 30 minutes / stand: 10 minutes / serves 6

¼ cup olive oil
3 tablespoons chopped shallots
1 tablespoon crushed red pepper
  Salt
¼ teaspoon garlic powder
¼ teaspoon chili powder
¼ teaspoon dried oregano
2 12-ounce pork tenderloins
2 large onions, cut into
  ¼-inch-thick slices
1 clove garlic, minced
1 teaspoon black pepper

1. For marinade, in a bowl combine 3 tablespoons of the olive oil, the shallots, crushed red pepper, ½ teaspoon salt, garlic powder, chili powder, and oregano. Coat pork tenderloins with the marinade. Cover and marinate in the refrigerator for 30 minutes.

2. Arrange hot coals around a drip pan. Test for medium-hot heat above the pan. Place meat on grill rack over pan. Cover; grill for 30 to 35 minutes or until an instant-read meat thermometer inserted in the thickest part of the tenderloin registers 155°F. Remove meat from grill. Cover meat with foil; let stand for 10 minutes.

3. Meanwhile, in another bowl combine onion slices, the remaining 1 tablespoon olive oil, and the garlic. Season with black pepper and a pinch of salt. Grill onions for 10 to 15 minutes or until tender, turning once.

4. To serve, slice pork and serve with onions.

G'S GOTTA-BE-QUICK TIP:------------------
TUCK UNDER THE THIN ENDS OF THE PORK
TENDERLOINS WHEN GRILLING SO THE MEAT
COOKS EVENLY.

SLOW-GRILLED ROSEMARY-GARLIC CHICKEN

prep: 15 minutes / marinate: 30 minutes / grill: 45 minutes / stand: 10 minutes / serves 4 to 6

1	3-pound broiler-fryer chicken
1½	cups olive oil
½	cup coarsely chopped fresh rosemary
6	garlic cloves, smashed
2	teaspoons cracked black pepper Kosher salt

1. Using heavy kitchen shears, cut through chicken on either side of the backbone. Remove backbone and discard. Flatten chicken with your hands. Place in a shallow baking dish. For marinade, in a small bowl combine olive oil, rosemary, garlic, and pepper. Pour marinade over chicken. Cover and marinate in the refrigerator for 30 minutes.

2. Drain chicken, discarding marinade. Season with salt. Place chicken, bone side down, on the rack of an uncovered grill directly over medium coals. Grill for 45 to 50 minutes or until an instant-read meat thermometer inserted in the center of an inside thigh muscle registers 180°F, turning once. Transfer to a cutting board; cover with foil. Let stand for 10 minutes. Cut into serving-size pieces.

G'S GOTTA-BE-QUICK TIP: ----------------
SERVE THIS CRISPY GRILLED CHICKEN WITH YOUR
FAVORITE DELI COLESLAW AND WARM DINNER ROLLS.

GRILLED GINGER CHICKEN

prep: 15 minutes / marinate: 1 to 24 hours / grill: 50 minutes / serves 6 to 8

¼   cup chopped garlic
2   tablespoons chopped shallots
2   teaspoons kosher salt
2   3- to 3½-pound whole broiler-fryer
      chickens, cut into pieces
      (see photo below)
¼   cup orange juice
¼   cup rum
¼   cup olive oil
1   tablespoon packed brown sugar
1   tablespoon soy sauce
1   1½-inch-long piece fresh ginger,
      finely chopped

1. In a small bowl combine garlic, shallots, and salt. Rub chicken pieces with garlic mixture. Place one cut-up chicken in each of two resealable plastic bags set in shallow bowls.

2. For marinade, in a bowl combine orange juice, rum, olive oil, brown sugar, soy sauce, and ginger. Pour half of the marinade over chicken in each bag. Seal bags. Marinate in the refrigerator for at least 1 hour or up to 24 hours.

3. Arrange medium-hot coals around a drip pan. Test for medium heat above the pan. Drain chicken, reserving marinade. Place chicken pieces, bone sides down, on grill rack over drip pan. Cover and grill for 30 minutes. Meanwhile, in a saucepan bring reserved marinade to a boil; reduce heat. Simmer for 5 minutes. Brush chicken with marinade; turn chicken pieces over. Grill for 20 to 30 minutes more or until chicken is done (170°F for breasts; 180°F for thighs and drumsticks), brushing frequently with marinade.

15-MINUTE-MARINATED CHICKEN

prep: 15 minutes / marinate: 15 minutes to 3 hours / grill: 12 minutes / serves 4

¼ cup Dijon mustard
1 tablespoon lemon juice
1 tablespoon lime juice
1½ teaspoons Worcestershire sauce
½ teaspoon dried rosemary
¼ teaspoon freshly ground black pepper
4 boneless, skinless chicken breast halves
Salt

1. In a small bowl combine Dijon mustard, lemon juice, lime juice, Worcestershire sauce, rosemary, and pepper; set aside.
2. Season chicken with salt. Spread mustard mixture on both sides of each chicken breast half. Place in a bowl; cover. Marinate in the refrigerator for at least 15 minutes or up to 3 hours.
3. Place chicken on the rack of an uncovered grill directly over medium coals. Grill for 12 to 15 minutes or until done (170°F), turning once.

𝒢'S GOTTA-BE-QUICK TIP: -----------------
SERVE THIS SUCCULENT CHICKEN WITH A SALAD MADE
FROM PACKAGED MIXED GREENS.

GRILLED JAMAICAN JERK CHICKEN

prep: 10 minutes / marinate: 30 minutes to 3 hours / grill: 35 minutes / serves 4

8 chicken drumsticks, skinned
3 tablespoons olive oil
2 tablespoons soy sauce
4½ teaspoons lemon juice
4 teaspoons Jamaican jerk seasoning
1 tablespoon honey

1. Using a sharp knife, score drumsticks by slashing at 1-inch intervals (see photo at left). Place in a resealable plastic bag set in a shallow bowl. For marinade, in a small bowl combine olive oil, soy sauce, lemon juice, jerk seasoning, and honey. Pour over chicken; seal bag. Marinate in the refrigerator for at least 30 minutes or up to 3 hours, turning occasionally.
2. Drain chicken, reserving marinade. Place chicken on the rack of an uncovered grill directly over medium coals. Grill for 35 to 45 minutes or until done (180°F), turning frequently and basting with reserved marinade up to the last 5 minutes of grilling. Discard any remaining marinade.

GRILLED TURKEY CUTLETS WITH RASPBERRY GLAZE

prep: 20 minutes / grill: 8 minutes / serves 4

1	tablespoon granulated sugar
1	tablespoon packed brown sugar
2	tablespoons sherry vinegar
½	cup raspberry jam or preserves
1	tablespoon chopped shallots
1	teaspoon shredded orange zest
1	clove garlic, minced
	Salt
	Ground white pepper
4	4- to 6-ounce turkey cutlets
	Garlic powder
	Onion powder
	Cayenne pepper
1	tablespoon olive oil

1. For raspberry glaze, in a saucepan stir granulated sugar and brown sugar into sherry vinegar; heat and stir until sugars are dissolved. Stir in raspberry jam, shallots, orange zest, and garlic. Bring to a boil; remove from heat. Season to taste with salt and white pepper; set aside.

2. Season turkey on both sides with salt, garlic powder, onion powder, and cayenne pepper. Drizzle both sides with olive oil.

3. Place turkey on the greased rack of an uncovered grill directly over medium coals. Grill for 8 to 9 minutes or until done (170°F), turning once.

4. To serve, arrange turkey pieces on a platter; brush with raspberry glaze.

TURKEY-SPINACH BURGERS

prep: 20 minutes / grill: 14 minutes / serves 10

1	8-ounce package frozen chopped spinach
2½	pounds ground uncooked turkey
1	cup fresh mushrooms, chopped
1	onion, chopped
2	eggs, lightly beaten
¼	cup ketchup
3	tablespoons chopped fresh parsley
2	tablespoons honey mustard
2	teaspoons dried Italian seasoning
1	teaspoon granulated garlic
1	teaspoon cumin
	Salt
	Black pepper
10	hamburger buns, split

1. In a medium saucepan cook spinach according to package directions; drain well. Squeeze out as much liquid as possible.

2. In a large bowl combine spinach, turkey, mushrooms, onion, eggs, ketchup, parsley, honey mustard, Italian seasoning, granulated garlic, and cumin. Season with salt and pepper. Shape into ten ½-inch-thick patties.

3. Place patties on the unheated rack of an uncovered grill directly over medium coals. Grill for 14 to 18 minutes or until done (165°F),* turning once. Serve in hamburger buns.

*NOTE: The internal color of a burger is not a reliable doneness indicator. A turkey patty cooked to 165°F is safe, regardless of color. To measure the doneness of a patty, insert an instant-read thermometer through the side of the patty to a depth of 2 to 3 inches.

GRILLED TUNA

prep: 15 minutes / grill: 4 minutes per ½-inch thickness of fish / serves 4

¼ cup (½ stick) unsalted
  butter, melted
1 tablespoon garlic powder
1 teaspoon chopped fresh basil
1 teaspoon lemon juice
½ teaspoon dried parsley flakes
  Pinch salt
4 5- to 6-ounce fresh tuna steaks
  Black pepper

1. In a small bowl combine butter, garlic powder, basil, lemon juice, parsley, and salt; set aside.
2. Rinse fish; pat dry with paper towels. Measure thickness of fish. Place fish on the greased rack of an uncovered grill directly over medium coals. Brush fish with half of the butter mixture and sprinkle with pepper. Grill for 4 to 6 minutes per ½-inch thickness of fish or until done. Halfway through grilling, turn fish; brush with the remaining butter mixture and sprinkle with pepper. Discard any remaining butter mixture. (Or preheat broiler. Place fish on the greased unheated rack of a broiler pan. Brush fish with half of the butter mixture and sprinkle with pepper. Broil 4 to 5 inches from heat for 4 to 6 minutes per ½-inch thickness of fish or until done, turning, brushing with butter, and sprinkling with pepper as above.)

GRILLED LEMON-AND-MINT SHRIMP

prep: 20 minutes / marinate: 5 minutes / grill: 9 minutes / serves 4

12 fresh jumbo shrimp in their shells
¼ cup chopped fresh mint
¼ cup lemon juice
  Olive oil
2 teaspoons minced garlic
1 tablespoon unsalted
  butter, softened
4 2-inch-thick slices French
  baguette
  Kosher salt
2 bunches arugula leaves
  Cracked black pepper

1. Clean shrimp, removing shells; use tip of sharp knife to remove veins. Pat dry with paper towels; set aside. For marinade, in a large bowl combine mint, lemon juice, ¼ cup olive oil, and 1 teaspoon of the garlic; add shrimp. Marinate for 5 minutes.
2. Meanwhile, combine butter and the remaining 1 teaspoon garlic. Spread butter mixture on both sides of bread slices.
3. Drain shrimp, discarding marinade. Thread shrimp on two or three 8- to 10-inch metal skewers. Season shrimp with salt. Place skewers on the grill rack of an uncovered grill directly over medium coals. Grill for 9 to 11 minutes or until shrimp are done and firm to the touch, turning once. Grill bread slices for the last 1 to 2 minutes of shrimp grilling or until lightly toasted, turning once.
4. Place toasted bread slices in the center of a large platter. Arrange shrimp around the edges of the platter. Place arugula leaves on top of bread slices. Drizzle lettuce with 2 teaspoons olive oil. Season with salt and pepper.

GRILLED HALIBUT WITH GARLIC AND THYME

prep: 10 minutes / grill: 4 minutes per ½-inch thickness of fish / serves 6

2	tablespoons lime juice
1	tablespoon olive oil
1	tablespoon chopped garlic
1	teaspoon chopped
	fresh rosemary
1	teaspoon chopped fresh thyme
½	teaspoon black pepper
¼	teaspoon garlic powder
6	4-ounce skinless fresh halibut
	fillets

1. In a small bowl combine lime juice, olive oil, garlic, rosemary, thyme, pepper, and garlic powder.
2. Rinse fish; pat dry with paper towels. Measure thickness of fish. Brush lime juice mixture on both sides of each fish fillet.
3. Place fish on the greased grill rack of an uncovered grill directly over medium coals. Grill for 4 to 6 minutes per ½-inch thickness of fish or until done, turning once.

GRILLED SWORDFISH WITH ORANGE-CILANTRO SAUCE

prep: 15 minutes / marinate: 1 to 2 hours / grill: 4 minutes per ½-inch thickness of fish / serves 4

1½	pounds fresh swordfish steaks
	or other firm fish steaks
	Salt
	Freshly ground black pepper
2	teaspoons olive oil
¼	cup chopped shallots
1	clove garlic, crushed
1	teaspoon orange marmalade
⅓	cup orange juice
2	tablespoons finely chopped
	fresh cilantro

1. Rinse fish; pat dry with paper towels. Measure thickness of fish. Season with salt and pepper. Place fish in a shallow baking dish; set aside.
2. For marinade, in a small nonstick skillet heat olive oil over medium heat. Add shallots and garlic; sauté about 5 minutes or until shallots and garlic are soft. Stir in orange marmalade. Stir in orange juice. Pour marinade over fish. Cover and marinate in the refrigerator for at least 1 hour or up to 2 hours.
3. Drain fish, discarding marinade. Place fish on the greased rack of an uncovered grill directly over medium coals. Grill for 4 to 6 minutes per ½-inch thickness of fish or until done. Divide fish among four dinner plates. Sprinkle with cilantro.

STRING BEAN, CANNELLINI BEAN, AND BELL PEPPER SALAD (RIGHT)
RECIPE ON PAGE 169

PECAN-AND-RAISIN BREAD PUDDING (LEFT)
RECIPE ON PAGE 187
POACHED PEARS WITH CINNAMON ICE CREAM (ABOVE)
RECIPE ON PAGE 182

CHEESE RAVIOLI TOPPED WITH SPICY
TOMATO AND SAUSAGE SAUCE
RECIPE ON PAGE 198

CORNISH GAME HEN THREE WAYS
RECIPE ON PAGE 199

EASY SEAFOOD JAMBALAYA (LEFT)
RECIPE ON PAGE 204

SMOKED HAM-AND-GRUYÈRE SANDWICHES (ABOVE)
RECIPE ON PAGE 68
CARAMEL-COATED PINEAPPLE (RIGHT)
RECIPE ON PAGE 188

VERMICELLI WITH SAUTÉED CABBAGE, CARROTS, AND
CHICKEN IN ASIAN DRESSING (LEFT)
RECIPE ON PAGE 86
WHITE BEANS WITH KIELBASA (ABOVE)
RECIPE ON PAGE 197

STRAWBERRY-AND-BANANA
MILK SHAKE
RECIPE ON PAGE 191

GRILLED BLACKENED SALMON

prep: 15 minutes / grill: 4 minutes per ½-inch thickness of fish / serves 4

4   6-ounce skinless fresh
    salmon fillets
1   tablespoon olive oil
    Sea salt
    Black pepper
4   teaspoons G's Blackening Spice
¼   cup (½ stick) unsalted butter
2   leeks, finely chopped
    Hot mashed potatoes

1. Rinse fish; pat dry with paper towels. Measure thickness of fish. Brush each fish fillet on both sides with olive oil; season with salt and pepper. Place fish on the greased rack of an uncovered grill directly over medium coals. Grill for 4 to 6 minutes per ½-inch thickness of fish or until done. Halfway through grilling, sprinkle fish with Blackening Spice; turn. Sprinkle the second side with Blackening Spice.

2. Meanwhile, in a medium sauté pan melt butter over medium heat. Add leeks; sauté about 5 minutes or until softened. Season with salt and pepper.

3. Serve fish with leeks and mashed potatoes.

WHOLE KING CRAB LEGS GRILLED WITH GARLIC BUTTER

prep: 30 minutes / grill: 11 minutes / serves 6

4   pounds whole king crab legs,
    split in half lengthwise
3   lemons, halved
    Kosher salt
1   pound (4 sticks) unsalted butter
3   tablespoons minced garlic
3   tablespoons chopped fresh thyme
2   tablespoons olive oil
1   teaspoon cracked white pepper

1. Rinse crab legs; pat dry with paper towels. Bring a large pot of water to a boil. Add crab legs, lemons, and 3 tablespoons kosher salt. Return to boiling; cook for 12 minutes. Drain crab legs.

2. In a saucepan heat butter, garlic, thyme, olive oil, and pepper until butter is melted. Season to taste with salt. Arrange crab legs on a large tray. Pour butter mixture over crab legs, turning crab legs to coat.

3. Place crab legs, cut sides down, on the rack of an uncovered grill directly over medium coals. Grill for 3 minutes; turn crab legs over. Grill for 3 minutes more; turn over. Grill for 5 to 7 minutes more or until done, turning frequently.

GINGER SALMON OVER MIXED GREENS SALAD

prep: 15 minutes / marinate: 20 minutes / grill: 4 minutes per ½-inch thickness of fish / serves 4

¼   cup honey

1   tablespoon soy sauce

1   4-inch-long piece fresh ginger, peeled and minced

4   cloves garlic, minced

4   6-ounce fresh salmon steaks or boneless, skinless salmon fillets

1   8- to 10-ounce package mixed torn greens

    Desired salad dressing

1. For marinade, in a bowl combine honey, soy sauce, ginger, and garlic. Rinse fish; pat dry with paper towels. Measure thickness of fish. Place fish in a baking dish; pour marinade over fish, turning fish to coat. Cover and marinate in the refrigerator for 20 minutes. Remove fish from marinade; reserve any remaining marinade.

2. Place fish on the greased rack of an uncovered grill directly over medium coals. Grill for 4 to 6 minutes per ½-inch thickness of fish or until done, turning and basting with reserved marinade once halfway through grilling. Discard any remaining marinade.

3. In a bowl toss greens with salad dressing. Divide greens among four salad plates. Top each serving with a piece of fish.

G'S GOTTA-BE-QUICK TIP: ------------------

TO PEEL FRESH GINGER QUICKLY WITH ONLY A LITTLE WASTE, SCRAPE THE SKIN OFF WITH THE EDGE OF A SPOON.

GRILLED SHRIMP, SPINACH, TOMATO, AND BELGIAN ENDIVE SALAD PITAS

prep: 25 minutes / grill: 5 minutes / serves 4

¼ cup fresh pink grapefruit juice
¼ cup olive oil
1 tablespoon honey
2 teaspoons stone-ground mustard
1 teaspoon chopped shallots
1 teaspoon chopped garlic
1 teaspoon lemon juice
   Pinch kosher salt
   Pinch black pepper
8 to 10 fresh large shrimp in their
      shells (about 8 ounces)
   G's Salt Seasoning
2 cups fresh baby spinach
      (2 ounces)
1 head Belgian endive, cut into
      ¼-inch-thick slices
½ cup cherry tomatoes, halved
2 whole wheat pita breads,
      halved crosswise

1. For vinaigrette, in a medium bowl whisk together grapefruit juice, 3 tablespoons of the olive oil, the honey, stone-ground mustard, shallots, garlic, lemon juice, salt, and pepper; set aside.

2. Clean shrimp, removing shells; use tip of sharp knife to remove veins. Pat dry with paper towels. In a medium bowl combine shrimp, the remaining 1 tablespoon olive oil, and Salt Seasoning to taste, tossing to coat shrimp well. Thread shrimp on two or three skewers. (If using wooden skewers, prevent burning while grilling by soaking them in cold water for at least 30 minutes before threading with shrimp.) Place skewers on the grill rack of an uncovered grill directly over medium coals. Grill for 5 to 8 minutes or until shrimp are done and firm to the touch, turning once.

3. In a large bowl toss together shrimp, spinach, Belgian endive, and tomatoes. Toss with vinaigrette to coat. Divide mixture among pita bread halves.

GRILLED SHRIMP WITH ROASTED GARLIC MARINADE

prep: 30 minutes / bake: 45 minutes / marinate: 2 to 3 hours / grill: 5 minutes / serves 4

2   medium bulbs garlic
1   tablespoon olive oil
1   cup orange juice
½   cup spicy honey mustard
2   tablespoons honey
1   teaspoon dried thyme
1   teaspoon dried rosemary
    Salt
1   pound fresh large shrimp
      in their shells
1   medium red bell pepper,
      seeded and cut into
      1-inch pieces
1   medium yellow bell pepper,
      seeded and cut into
      1-inch pieces
1   medium red onion,
      quartered and separated
    Black pepper
    Nonstick cooking spray
    Hot cooked couscous
      or brown rice

1. Heat oven to 375°F. Cut off the top of the garlic bulbs just enough to expose the individual cloves. Place bulbs in a small baking dish; drizzle with olive oil. Bake about 45 minutes or until garlic feels soft when squeezed. Cool. Squeeze garlic out of skins.

2. For marinade, in a blender or food processor combine roasted garlic, orange juice, honey mustard, honey, thyme, rosemary, and a pinch of salt. Cover and blend or process until smooth. Pour 1 cup of the marinade into a separate container; cover and refrigerate until serving time.

3. Clean shrimp, removing shells; use tip of sharp knife to remove veins. Pat dry with paper towels. In a resealable plastic bag set in a shallow bowl combine shrimp, bell peppers, and onion. Sprinkle with salt and black pepper. Pour the remaining marinade over shrimp; seal bag. Marinate in the refrigerator for at least 2 hours or up to 3 hours.

4. Drain shrimp and vegetables, discarding marinade. Alternately thread shrimp and vegetables onto four 8- to 10-inch skewers, leaving ¼-inch space between pieces. (If using wooden skewers, prevent burning while grilling by soaking them in cold water for at least 30 minutes before threading with shrimp and vegetables.) Coat the unheated grill rack of an uncovered grill with nonstick cooking spray. Place shrimp on grill rack directly over medium coals. Grill for 5 to 8 minutes or until shrimp are done and firm to the touch and vegetables are crisp-tender, turning once.

5. To serve, place skewers on a serving tray; drizzle with the reserved 1 cup marinade. Serve with hot cooked couscous or brown rice.

GRILLED VEGETABLE SALAD WITH
BALSAMIC VINAIGRETTE AND BABY SPINACH

prep: 25 minutes / grill: 25 minutes / serves 10

1 ear fresh corn with husks
1 large white onion
6 baby carrots
2 zucchini, quartered lengthwise
2 yellow squash,
    quartered lengthwise
2 large tomatoes, cored
    and halved crosswise
  Kosher salt
  Cracked white pepper
8 ounces fresh baby spinach
1 5- to 8-ounce package
    mesclun
¼ cup balsamic vinaigrette
    salad dressing

1. Peel back the husks on the corn, but do not remove. Remove corn silks. Rinse corn; pat dry with paper towels. Fold husks back around cob. Tie husk tops with 100%-cotton kitchen string; set aside. Slice onion into ½-inch-thick slices. If desired, insert a toothpick into the side of each onion slice to hold the rings together while grilling; set aside. Cut tops from baby carrots; peel and wash carrots. In a large saucepan bring a small amount of water to a boil; add salt. Add carrots; cook about 5 minutes or until almost tender. Drain; set aside.

2. Place corn, onion, baby carrots, zucchini, and yellow squash on the rack of an uncovered grill directly over medium coals. Add tomatoes, cut sides down. Grill vegetables until tender, removing the different vegetables as they are done. (Allow 3 to 5 minutes for the baby carrots, about 5 minutes for the tomatoes, 5 to 6 minutes for the zucchini and yellow squash, 8 to 10 minutes for the onion, and 25 to 30 minutes for the corn.) Cool vegetables. Cut corn from the cob; dice the remaining grilled vegetables.

3. In a large bowl combine all of the grilled vegetables. Season to taste with salt and white pepper. In another large bowl combine spinach and mesclun; add to vegetables, mixing well. Drizzle with balsamic vinaigrette salad dressing; toss to coat.

G'S GOTTA-BE-QUICK TIP: -----------------
IF YOU PREFER, USE 1 CUP FROZEN WHOLE KERNEL
CORN, THAWED, INSTEAD OF GRILLING THE CORN
ON THE COB.

GARLIC-ROASTED VEGETABLE MEDLEY

prep: 25 minutes / bake: 12 minutes / serves 10

3 tablespoons olive oil

12 cloves garlic, smashed

4 cups plum tomatoes, peeled and halved

4 zucchini, sliced

4 yellow squash, sliced

4 Japanese eggplant, sliced

2 red onions, cut in wedges

2 cups halved Brussels sprouts

8 ounces shiitake mushrooms, stems removed

Kosher salt

1 cup white wine

2 tablespoons unsalted butter, cut up

1. Preheat oven to 350°F. In a large roasting pan heat olive oil over medium heat. Add garlic; sauté until fragrant. Add tomatoes, zucchini, yellow squash, eggplant, red onions, Brussels sprouts, and mushrooms. Season with salt. Pour in wine; add butter. Bake for 12 to 15 minutes or until vegetables are crisp-tender.*

*NOTE: If you enjoy soft vegetables, bake for 10 minutes longer.

G'S GOTTA-BE-QUICK TIP: ----------------
THESE VEGETABLES ARE GOOD HOT OR COLD. TO
SERVE THEM COLD, DRIZZLE THEM WITH YOUR
FAVORITE VINAIGRETTE SALAD DRESSING AND
TEAM THEM—ANTIPASTO-STYLE—WITH ITALIAN
MEATS AND CHEESES.

BEER-SIMMERED BEANS

prep: 35 minutes / cook: 15 minutes / serves 4

4 ounces bacon, diced
1 large red onion, chopped
2 fresh jalapeño chile peppers,
   seeded and chopped*
4 cloves garlic, minced
1 12-ounce can beer
1 cup molasses
1 cup packed brown sugar
1 teaspoon dry mustard
1 teaspoon chili powder
1 teaspoon Worcestershire sauce
1 15- to 16-ounce can navy beans,
   rinsed and drained

1. In a medium pot cook bacon over medium to high heat until crispy. Drain bacon, reserving 1 tablespoon of the drippings. Return bacon and the 1 tablespoon drippings to pot. Add onion, jalapeño peppers, and garlic to the pot. Sauté about 7 minutes or until onion is soft.
2. Stir beer and molasses into onion mixture in pot. Bring to a boil. Stir in brown sugar, mustard, chili powder, and Worcestershire sauce. Return to a boil; reduce heat. Simmer for 5 minutes.
3. Stir in beans. Return to a boil; reduce heat. Simmer for 15 to 20 minutes or until desired consistency.

*NOTE: Because chile peppers contain volatile oils that can burn your skin and eyes, avoid direct contact with them as much as possible. When working with chile peppers, wear plastic or rubber gloves. If your bare hands do touch the peppers, wash your hands and nails well with soap and warm water.

SAUTÉED CORN WITH DICED BELL PEPPERS

start to finish: 15 minutes / serves 8

1 tablespoon olive oil
2 small red bell peppers, seeded
   and diced
1 teaspoon minced garlic
3 11-ounce cans sweet crisp whole
   kernel corn, drained
  Kosher salt
  Ground white pepper
1 tablespoon unsalted butter

1. In a medium sauté pan heat olive oil over medium heat. Add bell peppers and garlic. Sauté about 2 minutes or until peppers are softened. Stir in corn; cook for 3 minutes more. Season with salt and white pepper. Stir in butter until melted.

SUPER TASTY CHICKEN SALAD

prep: 15 minutes / chill: 1 to 4 hours / serves 6

2   cups cubed cooked chicken
1   10-ounce package frozen
      peas, thawed
¾   cup sliced celery
2   tablespoons minced garlic
1   tablespoon minced onion
2   teaspoons lemon juice
¾   cup ranch salad dressing
      G's Salt Seasoning

1. In a medium bowl combine chicken, peas, celery, garlic, onion, and lemon juice.
2. Add salad dressing, tossing to coat. Sprinkle with Salt Seasoning to taste. Cover and chill in the refrigerator for at least 1 hour or up to 4 hours.

G'S GOTTA-BE-QUICK TIP: -----------------

THIS SALAD IS A GREAT USE FOR LEFTOVER GRILLED CHICKEN. OR PICK UP A ROASTED BIRD FROM YOUR SUPERMARKET'S DELI COUNTER.

STRING BEAN, CANNELLINI BEAN, AND BELL PEPPER SALAD

prep: 25 minutes / grill: 8 minutes / serves 10

1 red bell pepper, halved
   and seeded
1 yellow bell pepper, halved
   and seeded
3 tablespoons olive oil
   Salt
1 pound fresh green
   beans, trimmed
2 15- to 16-ounce cans cannellini
   beans (white kidney beans),
   Great Northern beans, or navy
   beans, rinsed and drained
2 tablespoons capers, drained
2 anchovy fillets, finely chopped
2 tablespoons red wine vinegar
   Black pepper

1. Rub bell pepper pieces with 1 tablespoon of the olive oil. Place on the rack of an uncovered grill directly over medium coals. Grill for 8 to 10 minutes or until charred on all sides, turning frequently. Remove from grill; place in a resealable plastic bag. Seal bag. Let stand for 5 minutes. Peel peppers and slice into bite-size strips; set aside.

2. Meanwhile, in a large pot bring water to a boil; add a pinch of salt. Add green beans. Cover and cook for 10 to 15 minutes or until crisp-tender; drain. Cool in ice water. Drain again.

3. In a large bowl combine bell pepper strips, green beans, cannellini beans, capers, and anchovy fillets, tossing to combine. For dressing, in a small bowl whisk together the remaining 2 tablespoons olive oil and the red wine vinegar. Season to taste with salt and black pepper. Toss dressing with vegetables.

SEE PHOTO, PAGE 147

MARINATED CUCUMBER-AND-TOMATO SALAD

start to finish: 20 minutes / serves 6

2 long English cucumbers,
    thinly sliced
6 plum tomatoes, quartered
½ cup very thinly sliced red onion
¼ cup chopped fresh chives
½ cup red wine vinegar
3 tablespoons olive oil
4 teaspoons honey
1 tablespoon chopped shallots
1 teaspoon chopped fresh dill
   Salt
   Black pepper
4 ounces torn mixed spring greens

1. In a medium bowl combine cucumbers, plum tomatoes, onion, and chives. In another bowl whisk together red wine vinegar, olive oil, honey, shallots, and dill. Season with salt and pepper. Pour over vegetables, tossing to coat.

2. To serve, arrange greens on a platter. Spoon vegetables on top of greens.

TRI-COLOR PASTA SALAD

prep: 30 minutes / chill: 2 to 24 hours / serves 10

12 ounces dried tri-color corkscrew pasta
1 cup broccoli florets
3 tablespoons olive oil
2 medium zucchini, cut into ¼-inch-thick slices
1 large red bell pepper, seeded and cut into small chunks
1 large green bell pepper, seeded and cut into small chunks
½ cup halved cherry tomatoes
⅓ cup sliced radishes
3 scallions, chopped
Ranch or Italian salad dressing
G's Salt Seasoning
Garlic powder
Salt
Black pepper

1. In a pot bring water to a boil. Add corkscrew pasta; cook according to package directions, adding broccoli for the last 8 minutes of cooking. Drain pasta and broccoli; rinse with cool water. Drain again. In a large bowl toss pasta and broccoli with olive oil.

2. Stir in zucchini, bell peppers, cherry tomatoes, radishes, and scallions. Add 1 cup salad dressing, tossing to coat. Season to taste with Salt Seasoning, garlic powder, salt, and black pepper. Cover and chill in the refrigerator for at least 2 hours or up to 24 hours.

3. If desired, stir in more salad dressing before serving.

G'S GOTTA-BE-QUICK TIP: ----------------
INSTEAD OF CUTTING UP FRESH BROCCOLI, YOU CAN SUBSTITUTE 1 CUP FROZEN BROCCOLI FLORETS.

HONEY BBQ SAUCE

prep: 10 minutes / stand: 1 hour / makes about 1 cup

1   cup vegetable oil
¾   cup lemon juice
¼   cup honey
¼   cup soy sauce
4   teaspoons grated lemon zest
2   teaspoons dry mustard
      Salt
      Black pepper

1. In a bowl whisk together vegetable oil, lemon juice, honey, soy sauce, lemon zest, and mustard. Season with salt and pepper. Let stand at room temperature for 1 hour. Use to baste grilled or broiled chicken.

SUPER SIMPLE KICKED-UP BBQ SAUCE

start to finish: 35 minutes / makes about 2 cups

2   tablespoons unsalted butter
¼   cup finely chopped onion
¼   cup finely chopped garlic
¼   cup finely chopped shallots
1   cup water
1   cup ketchup
½   cup hot pepper sauce
2   tablespoons packed brown sugar
2   tablespoons vinegar
2   tablespoons
      Worcestershire sauce
2   tablespoons lemon juice
1   tablespoon crushed red pepper
1   teaspoon dry mustard
¼   teaspoon black pepper
1   teaspoon salt (optional)

1. In a medium saucepan melt butter over medium heat. Add onion, garlic, and shallots. Sauté until vegetables are soft. Stir in the water, ketchup, hot pepper sauce, brown sugar, vinegar, Worcestershire sauce, lemon juice, crushed red pepper, mustard, and black pepper. If desired, stir in salt. Bring to a boil; reduce heat. Simmer about 20 minutes or until mixture reaches desired consistency.

SANGRIA-STYLE REFRESHER

start to finish: 20 minutes / serves 12

8 cups grape juice
2 cups orange juice
½ cup sugar
2 peaches, pitted and
   cut into wedges
2 plums, pitted and cut
   into wedges
1 lemon, sliced
1 orange, sliced
8 cups club soda
   Ice cubes

1. In a large pitcher combine grape juice, orange juice, and sugar, stirring until the sugar dissolves. Add peaches, plums, lemon slices, and orange slices. Slowly add club soda, stirring to combine. Add ice and serve.

MAKE-AHEAD DIRECTIONS: If you like, you can mix the grape juice, orange juice, sugar, peaches, plums, lemon slices, and orange slices several days in advance. Cover and store in the refrigerator. To serve, add the club soda and ice cubes.

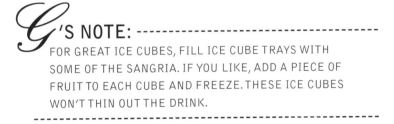

G'S NOTE: -----------------------------------
FOR GREAT ICE CUBES, FILL ICE CUBE TRAYS WITH
SOME OF THE SANGRIA. IF YOU LIKE, ADD A PIECE OF
FRUIT TO EACH CUBE AND FREEZE. THESE ICE CUBES
WON'T THIN OUT THE DRINK.

THE *sweetest* PART

After an amazing meal, what's better than good company and conversation—and a really great dessert? Enjoy every bite. – G

The best thing about dessert is that you don't have to make it from scratch.
Like many of the recipes in this chapter, you can buy half the stuff for an
amazing dessert already made and just put it all together at home. (My
Aunt Pat, for example, makes a great pound cake, so all we need to do
when we get together is buy some fresh berries and whipped cream.)
Dessert is my favorite time because you get to open up, relax your mind,
and let your body be free. As you clear the dinner dishes, try changing the
music to something a little upbeat. Or if you're lucky, maybe someone can
play a tune or two on the piano—and that cousin who always wants to sing
might just hit a note.

DESSERT—SWEET AND EASY—
IS THE PERFECT CAPPER FOR THE EVENING.

FRESH AND EASY FRUIT SALAD TOPPED
WITH NUTTY WHIPPED TOPPING

prep: 20 minutes / chill: 1 to 4 hours / serves 18

1   pint fresh strawberries, sliced
1   pound seedless grapes
2   cups cubed cantaloupe
1   11-ounce can mandarin orange
     sections, drained
4   kiwifruit, peeled and sliced
6   tablespoons sugar
½   teaspoon vanilla extract
1   cup whipping cream
1   teaspoon almond extract
1   cup finely chopped almonds
1   cup chocolate ice cream topping

1. In a large bowl combine strawberries, grapes, cantaloupe, mandarin oranges, and kiwifruit. Add 2 tablespoons of the sugar and the vanilla extract, tossing to combine. Cover and chill in the refrigerator for at least 1 hour or up to 4 hours.

2. Just before serving, in a chilled mixing bowl combine whipping cream, the remaining ¼ cup sugar, and the almond extract. Beat with an electric mixer on medium speed until soft peaks form. Serve fruit mixture in dessert dishes. Top each serving with some of the whipped cream mixture. Sprinkle each serving with almonds and drizzle with chocolate ice cream topping.

CINNAMON-APPLE TARTS

prep: 30 minutes / bake: 10 minutes / serves 12

2	tablespoons granulated sugar
1	tablespoon packed brown sugar
¼	teaspoon ground cinnamon
	Pinch ground nutmeg
½	of a 17.3-ounce package (1 sheet) frozen puff pastry, thawed
½	cup apricot jam or preserves
2	medium tart cooking apples (such as Granny Smith), cored and thinly sliced
	Vanilla ice cream

1. Preheat oven to 350°F. In a small bowl combine granulated sugar, brown sugar, cinnamon, and nutmeg; set aside.
2. Using a rolling pin, roll puff pastry to a 12×9-inch rectangle. Cut into twelve 3-inch squares. Prick pastry squares with a fork. Place squares on a baking sheet. Coat each square with a spoonful of apricot jam. Divide apple slices among squares, arranging nicely in the center of the squares. Sprinkle squares with sugar mixture.
3. Bake for 10 to 13 minutes or until apples are crisp-tender and pastry is golden brown. Serve hot with vanilla ice cream.

MIXED BERRY AND ICE CREAM SUNDAES

prep: 20 minutes / freeze: 4 hours / serves 24

Fruit Compote
Vanilla ice cream
Whipped cream

1. Place Fruit Compote in an 8×8×2-inch baking pan. Cover and freeze about 4 hours or until firm.
2. To serve, scoop ice cream into shot glasses or dessert dishes. Using the side of a spoon, scrape some of the frozen Fruit Compote to top each serving. Top with whipped cream.

FRUIT COMPOTE: In a bowl combine 1 cup fresh raspberries, 1 cup fresh blueberries, 1 cup halved fresh strawberries, and 2 tablespoons packed brown sugar. In a medium sauté pan melt 2 tablespoons unsalted butter over medium heat. Add berry mixture; sauté for 2 to 3 minutes. Serve warm or chilled. Makes 2½ cups.

VERY BERRY PIE

prep: 30 minutes / bake: 50 minutes / serves 8

Pastry for a Double-Crust
   Pie (recipe, page 181)
¼ cup granulated sugar
¼ cup packed brown sugar
3 tablespoons cornstarch
1½ cups fresh blueberries
1 cup fresh blackberries
1 cup fresh raspberries
1 cup fresh strawberries, halved
¼ teaspoon vanilla extract

1. Preheat oven to 375°F. On a lightly floured surface, use your hands to slightly flatten one ball of the Pastry for a Double-Crust Pie. Roll it from center to edge into a circle 12 inches in diameter. Wrap pastry circle around the rolling pin. Unroll pastry into a 9-inch pie plate. Ease pastry into pie plate without stretching. Roll remaining pastry ball into a circle 12 inches in diameter. Cut slits in pastry. Place in the refrigerator.

2. In a bowl combine granulated sugar, brown sugar, and cornstarch. Add blueberries, blackberries, raspberries, strawberries, and vanilla extract, tossing gently to coat.

3. Spoon berry mixture into pastry-lined pie plate. Trim bottom pastry to edge of pie plate. Place remaining pastry circle on top of berry mixture and seal edge, crimping as desired. To prevent overbrowning, cover edge of pie with foil. Bake for 25 minutes. Remove foil. Bake for 25 to 30 minutes more or until filling is bubbly and pastry is golden. Cool on a wire rack. To serve warm, let pie cool at least 2 hours.

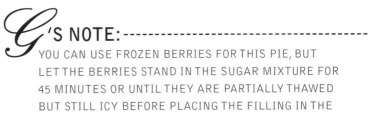

G'S NOTE:--

YOU CAN USE FROZEN BERRIES FOR THIS PIE, BUT LET THE BERRIES STAND IN THE SUGAR MIXTURE FOR 45 MINUTES OR UNTIL THEY ARE PARTIALLY THAWED BUT STILL ICY BEFORE PLACING THE FILLING IN THE PIECRUST. INCREASE THE BAKING TIME TO 50 MINUTES BEFORE REMOVING THE FOIL, THEN BAKE 25 TO 30 MINUTES MORE AFTER REMOVING THE FOIL.

SAUTÉED GRANNY SMITH APPLES WITH GRAND MARNIER®, PUFF PASTRY, AND VANILLA ICE CREAM

prep: 30 minutes / bake: 15 minutes / serves 12

6	tart cooking apples (such as Granny Smith), peeled and cored
¼	cup lemon juice
1	17.3-ounce package (2 sheets) frozen puff pastry, thawed
1	egg
1	tablespoon water
1	tablespoon canola oil
1	cup Grand Marnier® or other orange liqueur
½	cup granulated sugar
4	teaspoons unsalted butter
1	tablespoon packed brown sugar
1	tablespoon ground cinnamon
	Vanilla ice cream
	Fresh mint sprigs

1. Preheat oven to 350°F. Quarter apples lengthwise and place in a bowl of cold water. Stir in 2 tablespoons of the lemon juice; set aside. Line two baking sheets with parchment paper; set aside.

2. Using a 3½-inch round cutter, cut 12 circles from puff pastry. Place circles on parchment paper-lined baking sheets. In a small bowl beat together egg and the water. Brush mixture over puff pastry circles. Bake for 15 to 20 minutes or until circles are puffed and golden brown. Transfer to a wire rack; cool.

3. Meanwhile, drain apples; pat dry with paper towels. In a sauté pan heat canola oil over medium heat. Add apples; sauté for 5 minutes. Remove pan from heat; add Grand Marnier. Return to heat; heat until alcohol is burned off (stand back because the liqueur will flame up). Once flames have died down, stir in the remaining 2 tablespoons lemon juice, the granulated sugar, butter, brown sugar, and cinnamon. Sauté until apples are soft.

4. To serve, place a puff pastry circle in each of 12 cups. Spoon some of the apple mixture into each cup. Top each with a small scoop of ice cream. Garnish with fresh mint.

G 'S NOTE: --
PUTTING CUT APPLES INTO A MIXTURE OF WATER AND
LEMON JUICE WILL HELP KEEP THEM FROM TURNING
BROWN. BE SURE TO PAT THEM DRY WITH PAPER
TOWELS BEFORE SAUTÉING SO THEY BROWN NICELY
INSTEAD OF STEAM IN LIQUID.

APPLE-RAISIN PIE

prep: 30 minutes / bake: 1 hour / serves 8

Pastry for a Double-Crust Pie
3 tablespoons unsalted butter
8 tart cooking apples (such as
  Granny Smith), peeled and
  thinly sliced
¼ cup granulated sugar
¼ cup packed brown sugar
½ teaspoon ground cinnamon
¼ teaspoon ground nutmeg
⅛ teaspoon vanilla extract
⅛ teaspoon cornstarch
½ cup raisins

1. Preheat oven to 375°F. On a lightly floured surface, use your hands to slightly flatten one ball of the Pastry for a Double-Crust Pie. Roll it from center to edge into a circle 12 inches in diameter. Wrap pastry circle around the rolling pin. Unroll pastry into a 9-inch pie plate. Ease pastry into pie plate without stretching. Roll remaining pastry ball into a circle 12 inches in diameter. Cut slits in pastry. Place in the refrigerator.

2. In a large skillet melt the butter over medium heat; add apples. Stir in granulated sugar, brown sugar, cinnamon, nutmeg, and vanilla extract. Sauté about 5 minutes or until apples are soft. Stir in cornstarch. Let mixture cool. Stir in raisins.

3. Spoon apple mixture into pastry-lined pie plate. Trim bottom pastry to edge of pie plate. Place remaining pastry circle on top of apple mixture and seal edge, crimping as desired. To prevent overbrowning, cover edge of pie with foil. Bake for 40 minutes. Remove foil. Bake about 20 minutes more or until filling is bubbly and pastry is golden. Cool on a wire rack. To serve warm, let pie cool at least 2 hours.

PASTRY FOR A DOUBLE-CRUST PIE: In a bowl stir together 2½ cups all-purpose flour, 3 tablespoons granulated sugar, and 1 teaspoon salt. Using a pastry blender or fork, cut in 1 cup (2 sticks) cubed unsalted butter until the pieces are the size of small peas. In a small bowl beat together 1 egg and ¼ cup cold water. Sprinkle 1 tablespoon of the egg mixture over part of the flour mixture; toss with a fork. Push moistened pastry to side of bowl. Continue moistening flour mixture, using 1 tablespoon of the egg mixture at a time, until flour mixture is moistened. Divide pastry in half, forming two balls.

POACHED PEARS WITH CINNAMON ICE CREAM

prep: 35 minutes / stand: 10 minutes / chill: 2 to 24 hours / serves 4

4	pears, peeled
3	cups port wine
2	cups Chambord®
2	cups red wine
½	cup granulated sugar
½	cup packed brown sugar
1	tablespoon ground cinnamon
3	tablespoons cornstarch
1½	cups water
	Cinnamon ice cream
	Fresh mint sprigs

1. Stand pears upright in a large saucepan. Add port, Chambord, red wine, granulated sugar, brown sugar, and cinnamon. Bring to a boil; reduce heat. Simmer for 20 minutes. Remove from heat; cover and let stand for 10 minutes. Transfer to a bowl. Cover and chill in the refrigerator for at least 2 hours or up to 24 hours.

2. For pear sauce, in a screw-top jar combine cornstarch and ½ cup of the water; shake to combine. Use a slotted spoon to remove pears from poaching liquid. Drain pears well; set aside. Place poaching liquid in a saucepan. Stir cornstarch mixture into poaching liquid. Add the remaining 1 cup water. Bring to a boil; reduce heat. Cook and stir until thickened and bubbly.

3. To serve, place a pear in each of four chilled dessert dishes. Drizzle pears with warm pear sauce. Add a scoop of ice cream to each dessert dish. Garnish with mint.

SEE PHOTO, PAGE 149

G'S NOTES:----------------------------------
CHAMBORD® IS A FRENCH BLACK RASPBERRY LIQUEUR.
YOU CAN SUBSTITUTE KIRSCH OR ANOTHER BERRY-FLAVOR
LIQUEUR, IF YOU LIKE.

PEANUTTY DESSERT CASSEROLE

prep: 20 minutes / freeze: 7 hours / stand: 5 minutes / serves 12

1   8-ounce package chocolate
    cream-filled cookies, crushed
½   of an 8-ounce package vanilla
    cream-filled cookies, crushed
½   cup (1 stick) unsalted
    butter, melted
2   quarts vanilla ice cream
1   cup peanuts, crushed
½   cup cashews, crushed
2   cups powdered sugar
½   cup (1 stick) unsalted butter
1   5-ounce can evaporated milk
½   cup milk chocolate pieces
⅓   cup peanut butter pieces

1. In a bowl combine crushed cookies and the ½ cup melted butter. Press mixture into the bottom of a 13×9×2-inch baking dish. Place ice cream in a chilled bowl; stir to soften. Spread ice cream evenly over cookie layer in baking dish. Sprinkle ice cream with peanuts and cashews. Cover and freeze about 1 hour or until ice cream is firm.

2. Meanwhile, in a saucepan combine powdered sugar, ½ cup butter, the evaporated milk, milk chocolate pieces, and peanut butter pieces. Bring to a boil. Boil for 8 minutes, stirring occasionally. Remove from heat; cool completely. Spread cooled chocolate mixture over frozen dessert. Cover and freeze for at least 6 hours or until firm.

3. To serve, let dessert stand at room temperature for 5 to 10 minutes before cutting into rectangles.

MINI PEAR TARTS

prep: 30 minutes / chill: 30 minutes / bake: 30 minutes / serves 8

½ of a 17.3-ounce package (1 sheet) frozen puff pastry, thawed

4 Anjou pears, peeled, halved, and cored

½ cup sugar

¼ teaspoon ground cinnamon

¼ cup (½ stick) unsalted butter, cut into 16 cubes

1. Preheat oven to 375°F. On a floured surface, roll out puff pastry to less than ⅛ inch thick. Transfer to a baking sheet. Cover and chill for 30 minutes.

2. Meanwhile, using a hand slicer, cut pears into very thin slices. In a small bowl combine sugar and cinnamon. Line a second baking sheet with parchment paper; set aside.

3. Cut out eight 4-inch circles from pastry.* Transfer pastry circles to parchment paper-lined baking sheet. Place one cube of butter in the center of each circle. Top each butter cube with a spoonful of the sugar mixture. Arrange pear slices in a circle, leaving very little edge showing and stacking 2½ inches high to make a beehive shape. (Use the smaller slices at the top of the beehives.) Place a second butter cube on top of each beehive and sprinkle with some of the remaining sugar mixture. Bake about 30 minutes or until pears are tender and golden brown.

*NOTE: If you like, cut decorative shapes from the puff pastry scraps to bake and use another time.

G'S GOTTA-BE-QUICK TIP: ----------------

YOU CAN WRAP AND FREEZE THE TARTS ONCE THEY'RE STACKED AND SUGARED TO BAKE LATER.

HONEY-STRAWBERRY SHORTCAKES

start to finish: 30 minutes / serves 5

1	10.2-ounce package (5) large flaky biscuits
2	cups fresh strawberries, halved
¼	cup balsamic vinegar
¼	cup honey
1	tablespoon packed brown sugar
¼	cup whipping cream
1	teaspoon vanilla extract
½	cup sliced almonds, toasted
5	sprigs fresh mint

1. Bake biscuits according to package directions. Cool on wire rack.

2. In a bowl combine strawberries, balsamic vinegar, 2 tablespoons of the honey, and the brown sugar; set aside. In a chilled small mixing bowl combine whipping cream and vanilla extract. Beat with an electric mixer on medium speed until soft peaks form. Fold in the remaining 2 tablespoons honey and beat until stiff peaks form.

3. To assemble shortcakes, split biscuits in half horizontally. Place a biscuit bottom on each of five dessert plates. Divide strawberry mixture among biscuit bottoms. Top each with some of the whipped cream mixture. Top with biscuit tops. Sprinkle each shortcake with some of the almonds and garnish with mint.

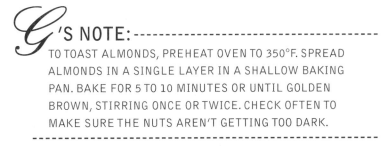

G'S NOTE: TO TOAST ALMONDS, PREHEAT OVEN TO 350°F. SPREAD ALMONDS IN A SINGLE LAYER IN A SHALLOW BAKING PAN. BAKE FOR 5 TO 10 MINUTES OR UNTIL GOLDEN BROWN, STIRRING ONCE OR TWICE. CHECK OFTEN TO MAKE SURE THE NUTS AREN'T GETTING TOO DARK.

FRUITY BREAD PUDDING WITH BRANDY BUTTER SAUCE

prep: 30 minutes / stand: 5 minutes / bake: 25 minutes / serves 12

¾ cup granulated sugar

3 tablespoons unsalted
   butter, softened
   Pinch ground nutmeg

3 eggs

2 tablespoons vanilla extract

3½ cups milk

4 cups sourdough or other heavy
   bread cut into 1-inch squares

4 cups raisin bread cut
   into 1-inch squares

1 cup fresh blueberries

1 cup sliced bananas

½ cup chopped walnuts

2 tablespoons granulated sugar

½ teaspoon ground cinnamon
   Brandy Butter Sauce

1. Preheat oven to 350°F. In a large mixing bowl combine the ¾ cup granulated sugar, the butter, and nutmeg. Beat with an electric mixer on medium to high speed until combined. Add eggs and vanilla extract. Beat for 2 to 3 minutes or until fluffy. Slowly stir in milk.

2 In a large bowl combine sourdough bread and raisin bread. Pour milk mixture over bread, mixing well to soak all bread cubes. Let stand for 5 minutes. Gently fold in blueberries, bananas, and walnuts. Transfer to a 3-quart baking dish. In a small bowl combine the 2 tablespoons granulated sugar and the cinnamon. Sprinkle evenly over mixture in baking dish. Drizzle mixture with ⅓ cup of the Brandy Butter Sauce.

3. Bake for 25 to 30 minutes or until a knife inserted in center comes out clean. To serve, reheat the remaining Brandy Butter Sauce. Serve bread pudding with sauce.

BRANDY BUTTER SAUCE: In a medium saucepan combine ½ cup packed brown sugar and 3 tablespoons butter. Heat over low heat until butter is melted. Remove from heat; stir in 1 cup heavy cream, 3 tablespoons brandy, and ¼ teaspoon vanilla extract. Bring to a boil, stirring continuously; reduce heat. Simmer for 5 to 10 minutes or until sauce is slightly thickened. Refrigerate if not using within 2 hours.

PECAN-AND-RAISIN BREAD PUDDING

prep: 25 minutes / bake: 25 minutes / serves 12

2   tablespoons unsalted butter
1   24-ounce package potato rolls
½   cup raisins
½   cup pecans
8   eggs
2   cups milk
1   14-ounce can sweetened
      condensed milk
1   cup heavy cream
2   teaspoons vanilla extract
1   cup sugar
    Pinch ground nutmeg
    Homemade caramel sauce
      or caramel ice cream
      topping, warmed
    Vanilla ice cream
    Fruit Compote (recipe, page 178)
    Fresh mint sprigs

1. Preheat oven to 350°F. Butter a 13×9×2-inch baking pan; set aside. Cut rolls in half and place in the baking pan. Sprinkle with raisins and pecans.

2. In a large bowl beat eggs well. Stir in milk, sweetened condensed milk, cream, and vanilla extract, mixing well. Stir in sugar and nutmeg until sugar is dissolved. Pour over mixture in baking pan.

3. Bake for 25 to 30 minutes or until pudding springs back when lightly touched and is golden brown.

4. To serve, divide pudding among 12 dessert plates. Drizzle each serving with some of the warmed caramel sauce. Add a scoop of ice cream to each plate. Top each scoop with some of the Fruit Compote. Garnish with mint.

SEE PHOTO, PAGE 148

BANANA FRENCH TOAST WITH VANILLA
BEAN ICE CREAM AND TOASTED ALMONDS

start to finish: 25 minutes / serves 4

2 eggs
¼ cup heavy cream
2 tablespoons vanilla extract
1 tablespoon vanilla syrup
1 teaspoon ground cinnamon
 Canola oil
4 slices egg bread (such as
 Hawaiian bread or challah),
 cut 1 inch thick
1 tablespoon unsalted butter
2 large bananas, sliced
2 tablespoons packed brown sugar
 Vanilla bean ice cream
½ cup sliced almonds, toasted
3 tablespoons powdered sugar

1. In a large bowl combine eggs, cream, vanilla extract, vanilla syrup, and cinnamon.
2. In a large sauté pan heat 1 tablespoon canola oil over medium heat. Dip each bread slice into egg mixture, letting it soak about 10 seconds on each side. Place bread slices in pan, cook about 4 to 6 minutes or until golden brown and crispy, turning once.
3. Meanwhile, in another sauté pan heat 1½ teaspoons canola oil and butter until butter is melted. Add bananas; sauté on high heat for 1 minute. Add brown sugar; sauté for 3 minutes more.
4. Place one slice of the French toast on each of four dessert plates. Top each with some of the banana mixture. Add two small scoops of ice cream to each. Sprinkle each serving with some of the almonds and powdered sugar.

CARAMEL-COATED PINEAPPLE

prep: 15 minutes / bake: 5 minutes / serves 4

½ cup packed brown sugar
1 tablespoon orange juice
1 tablespoon lemon juice
¼ teaspoon ground cinnamon
¼ teaspoon vanilla extract
1 fresh pineapple, peeled and
 cut into 8 slices
 Vanilla ice cream
 Fresh mint leaves

1. Preheat oven to 350°F. In a small bowl stir together brown sugar, orange juice, lemon juice, cinnamon, and vanilla extract until smooth. Spread sugar mixture on both sides of pineapple slices.
2. Place pineapple slices in a 3-quart rectangular baking dish. Bake about 5 minutes or until sugar mixture is melted and pineapple is heated through. On each of four dessert plates, place two slices of pineapple and a scoop of ice cream. Drizzle with some of the caramel sauce from baking dish. Garnish with mint.

SEE PHOTO, PAGE 157

CHOCOLATE-RUM POUND CAKE

prep: 25 minutes / stand: 30 minutes / bake: 25 minutes / cool: 10 minutes / serves 20 (2 cakes)

1	cup (2 sticks) unsalted butter
6	eggs
3	cups all-purpose flour
½	cup unsweetened cocoa powder
½	teaspoon baking powder
½	teaspoon salt
½	cup shortening
3	cups sugar
2	teaspoons rum extract
1	14-ounce can sweetened condensed milk

1. Allow butter and eggs to stand at room temperature for 30 minutes. Grease and lightly flour two 9×5×3-inch loaf pans; set pans aside. In a medium bowl stir together flour, cocoa powder, baking powder, and salt; set aside.

2. Preheat oven to 325°F. In a large mixing bowl cream butter and shortening with an electric mixer on medium to high speed for 30 seconds. Gradually add sugar, beating about 10 minutes or until light and fluffy. Beat in rum extract. Add eggs, one at a time, beating 1 minute after each addition and scraping bowl frequently. Alternately add flour mixture and sweetened condensed milk to butter mixture, beating on low to medium speed after each addition just until combined. Divide batter between prepared pans.

3. Bake for 25 to 30 minutes or until a wooden toothpick inserted near the centers comes out clean. Cool cakes in pans on wire racks for 10 minutes. Remove from pans; cool thoroughly on wire racks.

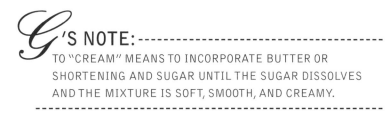

G'S NOTE:

TO "CREAM" MEANS TO INCORPORATE BUTTER OR SHORTENING AND SUGAR UNTIL THE SUGAR DISSOLVES AND THE MIXTURE IS SOFT, SMOOTH, AND CREAMY.

COOKIE ICE CREAM SANDWICHES

prep: 30 minutes / chill: 2 to 24 hours / bake: 10 minutes / freeze: 2 hours / stand: 5 minutes / 8 sandwiches

1 cup (2 sticks) unsalted butter, softened
1 cup granulated sugar
1 cup packed brown sugar
1½ teaspoons salt
1 teaspoon baking soda
2 eggs
1 cup sour cream
1 teaspoon vanilla extract
6 cups all-purpose flour
½ cup semisweet chocolate pieces
½ cup peanut butter pieces
1 quart vanilla ice cream

1. In a large mixing bowl beat butter with an electric mixer on medium to high speed for 30 seconds. Add granulated sugar, brown sugar, salt, and baking soda. Beat until mixture is combined. Beat in eggs, sour cream, and vanilla extract until combined. Beat in as much of the flour as you can with the mixer. Stir in remaining flour. Stir in chocolate pieces and peanut butter pieces. Cover and chill in the refrigerator for at least 2 hours or up to 24 hours.

2. Preheat oven to 350°F. On a lightly floured surface, roll dough, half at a time, until ¼ inch thick. Using a 3-inch round cookie cutter, cut dough into circles. (Because you will be making sandwiches with these cookies, be sure to cut out an even number.) Place circles 1 inch apart on ungreased cookie sheets. Bake about 10 minutes or until edges are firm (do not allow cookies to get brown and hard). Transfer to wire racks; cool.

3. Place ice cream in a chilled bowl; stir to soften. For each sandwich, place a scoop of vanilla ice cream on the flat side of a cookie, smoothing to make a flat surface; top with another cookie, flat side down. Wrap in plastic wrap. Freeze at least 2 hours.

4. To serve, let sandwiches stand at room temperature for 5 minutes.

STRAWBERRY-AND-BANANA MILK SHAKE

start to finish: 10 minutes / serves 6

3   large bananas, sliced
12 large strawberries, sliced
3   cups whole milk
2   scoops vanilla ice cream
    Whipped cream (optional)
    Fresh mint sprigs (optional)

1. In a blender combine bananas, strawberries, milk, and ice cream. Cover and blend until smooth. Pour into six glasses. If desired, top each glass with whipped cream and garnish with mint.

SEE PHOTO, PAGE 160

LUSCIOUS BLUEBERRY PIE

prep: 30 minutes / bake: 50 minutes / serves 8

    Pastry for a Double-Crust Pie
    (recipe, page 181)
4   cups frozen blueberries,
    thawed and drained
¼   cup packed brown sugar
3   tablespoons cornstarch
⅛   teaspoon vanilla extract
1   tablespoon unsalted butter,
    cut up

1. Preheat oven to 325°F. On a lightly floured surface, use your hands to slightly flatten one ball of the Pastry for a Double-Crust Pie. Roll it from center to edge into a circle 12 inches in diameter. Wrap pastry circle around the rolling pin. Unroll pastry into a 9-inch pie plate. Ease pastry into pie plate without stretching. Roll remaining pastry ball into a circle 12 inches in diameter. Cut slits in pastry. Place in the refrigerator.

2. In a bowl combine blueberries, brown sugar, cornstarch, and vanilla extract until thoroughly mixed.

3. Spoon berry mixture into pastry-lined pie plate. Top with butter. Trim bottom pastry to edge of pie plate. Place remaining pastry circle on top of berry mixture and seal edge, crimping as desired. To prevent overbrowning, cover edge of pie with foil. Bake for 25 minutes. Remove foil. Bake for 25 to 30 minutes more or until filling is bubbly and pastry is golden. Cool on a wire rack. To serve warm, let pie cool at least 2 hours.

G'S GOTTA-BE-QUICK TIP: ----------------
IF YOU PREFER, USE DRAINED CANNED BLUEBERRIES
INSTEAD OF THE FROZEN BERRIES.

MAKE SOME, BUY SOME

Make it easy on yourself, especially when you're cooking for the clan. In half the time, you'll toss that apron aside and be ready to eat. – G

Family gatherings are some of my favorite times because you don't have the usual pressures of having to cook everything. The recipes in this chapter are for anyone who's on-the-go and still wants to make a great meal. Truth be told, not everybody has time to raise a family, pick up the house—and then make and take a meal to Mom's for family night. That's why going to the store, picking up some things, and then adding your own touches is such a great idea. (People do it all the time—they just don't tell you!)

IT'S OK TO MIX IT UP IN THE KITCHEN: A LITTLE LOVE FROM THE STORE AND A LITTLE LOVE FROM YOUR HOME.

EASY BEEF STROGANOFF

prep: 20 minutes / cook: 27 minutes / serves 8

1½ to 2 pounds beef rib-eye
    steak, diced
    Kosher salt
    Black pepper
2 tablespoons olive oil
1 tablespoon chopped garlic
1 tablespoon chopped shallots
1 medium onion, diced
1 10¾-ounce can condensed
    cream of mushroom soup
¼ cup canned beef gravy
2 sprigs fresh thyme, chopped
1 tablespoon sour cream
    Hot mashed potatoes

1. Season meat with salt and pepper. In a large nonstick skillet heat 1 tablespoon of the olive oil over medium-high heat. Add half of the meat; cook until brown on all sides. Remove meat from skillet. Repeat with remaining 1 tablespoon olive oil and meat. Remove meat from skillet. Add garlic and shallots to skillet; sauté for 2 minutes. Stir in onion; sauté about 5 minutes or until soft.

2. Stir cream of mushroom soup into skillet. Stir in beef gravy and thyme. Simmer about 10 minutes or until mixture starts to thicken. Return meat to skillet; heat through. Finish with sour cream. Serve with mashed potatoes.

G'S GOTTA-BE-QUICK-TIP: ----------------
FOR AN EVEN FASTER DISH, USE PURCHASED BEEF
STIR-FRY STRIPS INSTEAD OF THE RIB-EYE STEAK.

GRILLED BBQ PORK LOIN WITH WILTED SPINACH AND BAKED SWEET POTATOES

prep: 20 minutes / bake: 30 minutes / stand: 5 minutes / serves 8

4   medium sweet potatoes, sliced
    Nonstick or olive oil cooking spray
8   slices boneless pork loin, cut ¼ to ½ inch thick
1   teaspoon G's Salt Seasoning
½   teaspoon cumin
1   cup barbecue sauce
4½ teaspoons olive oil
4½ teaspoons chopped garlic
2   6-ounce bags fresh baby spinach
    Salt
    Coarsely ground black pepper

1. Preheat oven to 375°F. Arrange sweet potatoes in a shallow baking pan. Spray with nonstick cooking spray. Bake for 25 to 30 minutes or until tender. Set aside.

2. Place pork slices in a medium bowl. Sprinkle with Salt Seasoning and cumin. Add ½ cup of the barbecue sauce, tossing to coat. Let stand for 5 to 10 minutes.

3. Spray an unheated grill pan with nonstick cooking spray. Heat over medium to high heat. Using paper towels, wipe off excess barbecue sauce from meat. Add meat to grill pan; cook about 4 minutes or until cooked through, turning once. Transfer pork to a baking sheet. Drizzle with remaining ½ cup barbecue sauce. Bake for 5 minutes.

4. In a large nonstick skillet heat olive oil over medium-high heat. Add garlic; sauté garlic until it starts to brown. Add a handful of spinach at a time, turning over with tongs until it starts to go limp. Continue adding spinach until all is wilted. Season to taste with salt and pepper. Serve pork loin with spinach and sweet potatoes.

HAM-AND-CHEESE BREAKFAST DROP BISCUITS

prep: 20 minutes / bake: 8 minutes / makes 10 to 12 biscuits

2 cups packaged biscuit mix
4 ounces thinly sliced ham, diced
6 slices Swiss cheese, diced
¼ cup chopped fresh chives

1. Preheat oven according to package directions for biscuit mix. In a large bowl prepare biscuit mix according to package directions. Stir in ham, Swiss cheese, and chives.
2. Using a tablespoon, drop 10 to 12 spoonfuls of batter onto an ungreased baking sheet. Bake for 8 to 10 minutes or until golden brown. Serve warm.

G'S GOTTA-BE-QUICK TIP:
USE KITCHEN SCISSORS TO CUT THE CHIVES INTO SHORT LENGTHS.

WHITE BEANS WITH KIELBASA

start to finish: 25 minutes / serves 8

1 tablespoon olive oil
1 pound turkey kielbasa, coarsely chopped
1 small onion, chopped
4 cloves garlic, minced
2 15- to 15.8-ounce cans Great Northern beans, rinsed and drained
1½ cups chicken stock
1 teaspoon salt
  Black pepper
2 tablespoons chopped fresh parsley

1. In a large skillet heat olive oil over medium-high heat. Add kielbasa, onion, and garlic; sauté about 5 minutes or until sausage is done.
2. Stir in beans, chicken stock, and salt. Bring to a boil; reduce heat to medium-low. Simmer for 2 to 3 minutes, stirring often. Season to taste with pepper. Stir in parsley.

SEE PHOTO, PAGE 159

G'S NOTE:
THIS BEAN-AND-SAUSAGE COMBO IS DELICIOUS OVER HOT COOKED PENNE.

CHEESE RAVIOLI TOPPED WITH
SPICY TOMATO AND SAUSAGE SAUCE

start to finish: 40 minutes / serves 8

1 pound uncooked hot Italian
  sausage, casings removed
  (see photo below)
1 large yellow bell pepper,
  seeded and chopped
1 medium onion, chopped
2 tablespoons chopped garlic
1 28-ounce can diced
  tomatoes, undrained
1 teaspoon dried basil
1 teaspoon dried oregano
1 cup white wine
1 6-ounce can tomato paste
1 16-ounce package frozen
  cheese ravioli
  Fresh oregano leaves
  Salt
  Black pepper
1 cup grated Parmesan cheese

1. For sauce, in a large deep skillet sauté sausage, bell pepper, onion, and garlic over medium heat until sausage is brown and vegetables are tender, breaking up sausage with a spoon while it cooks. Drain off fat.

2. Stir in undrained tomatoes, basil, and dried oregano. Stir in wine. Bring to a boil; reduce heat. Simmer for 10 minutes. Slowly stir in tomato paste. Simmer for 10 minutes more.

3. Meanwhile, in a large pot bring water to a boil; add salt. Add ravioli; cook according to package directions. Drain ravioli. Spoon sauce over ravioli. Garnish with oregano leaves. Season to taste with salt and pepper. Serve with Parmesan cheese.

SEE PHOTO, PAGE 150

CORNISH GAME HEN THREE WAYS

prep: 15 minutes / roast: 1 hour / serves 6

3 1¼- to 1½-pound rock
    Cornish game hens
2 tablespoons G's Blackening
    Spice
2 tablespoons G's Lemon
    Pepper Seasoning
1 tablespoon chopped
    fresh rosemary
1 tablespoon chopped fresh thyme
1 teaspoon minced garlic
    Kosher salt
    Cracked black pepper

1. Preheat oven to 375°F. Line a shallow roasting pan with foil;
   set aside. Season one of the game hens all over with Blackening
   Spice. Season another game hen all over with the Lemon Pepper
   Seasoning. Season the third all over with rosemary, thyme,
   garlic, salt, and pepper. Place game hens, breast sides up, in
   pan; twist wing tips under backs.
2. Roast, uncovered, for 1 to 1¼ hours or until an instant-read
   thermometer inserted into the thigh of each hen registers 180°F.

SEE PHOTO, PAGE 152-153

G'S GOTTA-BE-QUICK TIP:-----------------
YOU CAN SEASON THE GAME HENS WITH ALL THREE OR
JUST ONE OF THE SPICE BLENDS.

CHICKEN WITH CREAMY GRAVY

start to finish: 35 minutes / serves 6

1 tablespoon olive oil
6 boneless, skinless chicken
    breast halves
2 tablespoons unsalted butter
2 tablespoons chopped garlic
2 tablespoons chopped shallots
3 tablespoons all-purpose flour
1 cup chicken stock
2 cups milk
½ cup heavy cream
¼ cup white wine
    Salt
    Black pepper
    Hot mashed potatoes
      or hot cooked rice

1. In a very large skillet heat olive oil over medium heat. Add
   chicken; cook for 8 to 12 minutes or until done (170°F), turning
   once. Set aside.
2. In a large skillet melt butter over medium heat. Add garlic and
   shallots; sauté until shallots are soft. Stir in flour; cook and
   stir until mixture turns light brown and bubbles. Slowly pour in
   chicken stock, continuing to stir so lumps do not form. Slowly
   add milk and cream. Slowly add wine. Simmer mixture until
   desired consistency. Season to taste with salt and pepper.
3. Add chicken to skillet and simmer until chicken is heated
   through. Serve with mashed potatoes or hot cooked rice.

GARLIC AND CHICKEN PIZZA

prep: 20 minutes / stand: 1 hour / bake: 10 minutes / serves 2 as main dish or 8 as appetizer

1   tomato, chopped
3   tablespoons olive oil
2   tablespoons balsamic vinegar
4   cloves garlic, chopped
1   teaspoon chopped fresh basil
     Salt
     Black pepper
2   tablespoons chopped shallots
1   12-inch Italian bread shell (such
       as Boboli brand)
4   ounces diced cooked
       chicken breast
1   cup shredded mozzarella cheese
½   cup grated Parmesan cheese

1. Preheat oven to 375°F. In a bowl combine tomato, olive oil, balsamic vinegar, garlic, and basil. Season with salt and pepper. Let stand at room temperature for 1 hour. Drain tomato mixture.

2. Spread tomato and shallots on bread shell. Top with chicken, mozzarella cheese, and Parmesan cheese.

3. Bake for 10 to 12 minutes or until cheese is melted and edge of pizza is light brown.

SAUSAGE PINWHEELS

prep: 15 minutes / freeze: 30 minutes / bake: 20 minutes / serves 6

     Nonstick cooking spray
½   of a 17.3-ounce package (1 sheet)
       frozen puff pastry, thawed
6   ounces bulk turkey sausage
     Salt
     Black pepper

1. Preheat oven to 400°F. Line a baking sheet with parchment paper. Spray parchment paper with nonstick cooking spray. Set aside.

2. On a cutting board lay out puff pastry; spread with sausage. Sprinkle with salt and pepper. Starting at one short end, make a tight tuck and start to roll up evenly, keeping the roll tight until completely rolled up. Wrap in plastic wrap and place in the freezer about 30 minutes or until nice and firm.

3. Cut pastry roll into ½-inch-thick slices. Place slices, cut sides down, on prepared baking sheet. Bake about 20 minutes or until puffed and brown.

SAUTÉED CHICKEN WITH ELBOW PASTA AND MUSHROOM CREAM SAUCE

start to finish: 25 minutes / serves 6

Kosher salt

1 16-ounce package dried elbow macaroni

2 tablespoons unsalted butter

Cracked white pepper

1 tablespoon olive oil

6 8-ounce boneless, skinless chicken breast halves

3 10¾-ounce cans condensed cream of mushroom soup

2 cups water

1. In a large pot bring water to a boil; add salt. Add elbow macaroni; cook according to package directions. Drain; return to hot pot. Toss with butter. Season to taste with salt and white pepper. Keep warm.

2. Meanwhile, in a large sauté pan heat olive oil over medium heat. Add chicken; cook for 8 to 12 minutes or until done (170°F), turning once. Stir in cream of mushroom soup and the water. Bring to boiling; reduce heat to low. Simmer for 5 minutes.

3. To serve, divide pasta among six dinner plates; top each serving with a piece of chicken. Spoon some of the sauce from the skillet over each serving.

G'S GOTTA-BE-QUICK TIP:----------------
TO SPEED UP THIS RECIPE, USE A ROASTED CHICKEN
FROM THE DELI IN PLACE OF THE CHICKEN BREAST
HALVES. REMOVE THE CHICKEN FROM THE BONES;
DISCARD BONES. COARSELY SHRED THE CHICKEN AND
SIMMER IN THE SAUCE.

QUICK-AND-EASY CHICKEN NOODLE SOUP

prep: 15 minutes / cook: 20 minutes / serves 6

½ of a roasted chicken from the deli
4 cups chicken stock
1 9- to 10-ounce package
   frozen peas
½ of a 10-ounce bag
   shredded carrots
1 onion, diced
2 tablespoons olive oil
1 tablespoon chopped garlic
1 tablespoon chopped shallots
  Salt
  Black pepper
8 ounces dried egg noodles

1. Remove chicken from bones; discard bones. Chop chicken into bite-size pieces.
2. In a large pot combine chicken, chicken stock, peas, carrots, onion, olive oil, garlic, and shallots. Season with salt and pepper. Bring to a boil; add noodles. Return to boiling; simmer for 15 minutes.

QUICK-AND-EASY CHICKEN-PESTO PIZZA

start to finish: 15 minutes / serves 2 as main dish or 8 as appetizer

½ cup purchased basil pesto
1 12-inch Italian bread shell (such as Boboli brand)
1 9-ounce package frozen cooked chicken breast strips, thawed
½ cup shredded mozzarella cheese
1 cup halved cherry tomatoes

1. Preheat oven to 450°F. Spread pesto over bread shell. Arrange chicken pieces on top of pesto. Sprinkle with mozzarella cheese.
2. Bake for 5 minutes; top pizza with tomatoes. Bake for 3 to 5 minutes more or until cheese is melted and edge of pizza is lightly brown.

CREAMED CHICKEN AND RICE WITH SWEET PEAS

start to finish: 25 minutes / serves 8

4   6-ounce boneless, skinless
    chicken breast halves,
    cut into small pieces
    Kosher salt
    Cracked white pepper
¼   cup olive oil
2   10¾-ounce cans condensed
    cream of chicken soup
1   cup water
1   10-ounce package frozen
    sweet peas, thawed
3   tablespoons lemon juice
2   tablespoons unsalted butter
1   teaspoon minced garlic
6   cups hot cooked rice
    (unseasoned)

1. Season chicken with salt and pepper. In a medium sauté pan heat 1 tablespoon of the olive oil over medium heat. Add chicken; sauté about 7 minutes or until done. Stir in cream of chicken soup and the water. Bring to a boil; reduce heat to low. Simmer for 5 minutes. Stir in peas.

2. While chicken cooks, add the remaining 3 tablespoons olive oil, the lemon juice, butter, and garlic to hot cooked rice, tossing to coat.

3. To serve, spoon rice mixture onto a platter; top with chicken mixture.

G'S GOTTA-BE-QUICK TIP:
INSTEAD OF COOKING THE RICE, USE TWO 8.8-OUNCE POUCHES OF COOKED BUTTERY-FLAVOR RICE HEATED ACCORDING TO PACKAGE DIRECTIONS. OMIT THE 3 TABLESPOONS OLIVE OIL, THE LEMON JUICE, BUTTER, AND GARLIC.

EASY SEAFOOD JAMBALAYA

prep: 20 minutes / soak: 45 minutes / cook: 10 minutes / serves 8

6	fresh clams
6	fresh mussels
6	fresh shrimp in their shells
6	ounces skinless fresh salmon
6	ounces skinless fresh sea bass
4	ounces fresh sea or bay scallops
2	tablespoons olive oil
1	small green bell pepper, seeded and diced
3	cups white wine
6	plum tomatoes, crushed
2	tablespoons tomato paste
8	cups hot cooked rice (unseasoned)
2	tablespoons unsalted butter
	Kosher salt
	Ground white pepper

1. Scrub clams and mussels under cold running water; remove beards from mussels. Soak clams and mussels in cold salted water for 15 minutes; drain and rinse. Repeat twice more; set aside. Clean shrimp, removing shells; use tip of sharp knife to remove veins. Pat dry with paper towels. Set aside. Rinse salmon, sea bass, and scallops. Pat dry with paper towels. Set aside.

2. In a large sauté pan heat olive oil over medium heat. Add bell pepper; sauté for 2 minutes. Stir in wine, tomatoes, and tomato paste (see photo below). Bring to a boil. Add clams and mussels. Reduce heat. Cover and simmer for 3 minutes. Add shrimp, salmon, sea bass, and scallops. Cover and simmer about 5 minutes more or until seafood is done. Remove seafood from pan; keep warm.

3. Stir rice and butter into tomato mixture in pan. Season to taste with salt and white pepper. Serve with seafood.

SEE PHOTO, PAGE 154

FETTUCCINE AND ALFREDO SAUCE WITH SHRIMP

start to finish: 25 minutes / serves 6

16 to 20 fresh colossal shrimp in
     their shells (about 1 pound)
     Kosher salt
     Black pepper
1   16-ounce package
     dried fettuccine pasta
1   tablespoon olive oil
1   16-ounce jar Alfredo pasta sauce
½   cup grated Parmesan cheese
3   tablespoons unsalted butter
2   cloves garlic, chopped
     Chopped fresh parsley

1. Clean shrimp, removing shells; use tip of sharp knife to remove veins. Pat dry with paper towels. Season with salt and pepper. Set aside. In a large pot bring water to a boil; add salt. Add fettuccine; cook according to package directions. Drain pasta; toss with olive oil. Return to hot pot. Keep warm.

2. For Alfredo sauce, in a large saucepan combine Alfredo pasta sauce, Parmesan cheese, and half of the butter. Cook and stir over low heat until smooth and heated through.

3. In another saucepan melt the remaining butter over medium heat. Add garlic; sauté until fragrant. Add shrimp; sauté for 2 to 3 minutes or until shrimp is done and firm to the touch. Stir shrimp mixture into Alfredo sauce; toss shrimp and sauce with pasta. Sprinkle pasta with parsley.

QUICK CHEESE-AND-SPINACH RAVIOLI BAKE

prep: 10 minutes / bake: 30 minutes / serves 8

1 26-ounce jar tomato-base
 pasta sauce (any flavor)
1 30-ounce package frozen
 large cheese ravioli,
 thawed and drained
1 10-ounce package frozen
 spinach, thawed and drained
2 cups shredded mozzarella cheese
½ cup grated Romano cheese

1. Preheat oven to 350°F. Lightly grease a 3-quart rectangular baking dish. Spoon in about one-third of the pasta sauce. Arrange twelve ravioli on top. Top with spinach, 1 cup of the mozzarella cheese, and ¼ cup of the Romano cheese.
2. Spread half of the remaining pasta sauce on top of the spinach. Top with the remaining ravioli, the rest of the pasta sauce, the remaining 1 cup mozzarella cheese, and the remaining ¼ cup Romano cheese. Cover with foil.
3. Bake for 25 minutes. Uncover; bake for 5 to 10 minutes more or until bubbly.

WARM CHEDDAR CHEESE GRITS WITH SHRIMP, PANCETTA, AND SCALLIONS

start to finish: 35 minutes / serves 8

8	ounces fresh medium shrimp in their shells
4	cups water
1½	cups regular grits (not quick-cooking)
½	cup diced pancetta
1	tablespoon olive oil
1	cup shredded mild cheddar cheese
2	tablespoons unsalted butter
1	teaspoon kosher salt
½	teaspoon ground white pepper
½	cup sliced scallions

1. Clean shrimp, removing shells; use tip of sharp knife to remove veins. Pat dry with paper towels. Set aside. In a large saucepan bring the water and grits to a boil; reduce heat. Simmer for 15 to 20 minutes or until tender.

2. Meanwhile, in a large sauté pan sauté pancetta over medium heat about 12 minutes or until crispy. Remove from pan; set aside. Add olive oil to pan; heat over medium heat. Add shrimp; sauté about 2 minutes or until shrimp are done and firm to the touch. Remove shrimp from pan; set aside.

3. Add pancetta, cheddar cheese, butter, salt, and white pepper to grits, stirring until cheese and butter are melted. Transfer to a serving dish; top with shrimp and scallions.

SEE PHOTO, PAGE 45

SIMPLE STRAWBERRY SHORTCAKE

start to finish: 15 minutes / serves 8

1   10¾-ounce frozen pound
    cake, thawed
1   cup whipping cream
1   teaspoon vanilla extract
2   tablespoons powdered sugar
2   cups frozen sweetened sliced
    strawberries, thawed
2   cups fresh strawberries, sliced
8   whole fresh strawberries
    Fresh mint sprigs

1. Slice pound cake into 16 slices; set aside. In a chilled mixing bowl combine whipping cream and vanilla extract. Beat with an electric mixer on medium speed, slowly adding powdered sugar; beat until stiff peaks form. Set aside.

2. To serve, place one slice of the pound cake on each of eight dessert dishes. Top each pound cake slice with some of the frozen sliced strawberries and a scoop of whipped cream. Add another slice of the pound cake. Top each with some of the fresh sliced strawberries and another scoop of whipped cream. Garnish each with a whole strawberry and a mint sprig.

G'S NOTE:

TO MAKE THESE SHORTCAKES TRULY SPECTACULAR, USE A LOAF OF CHOCOLATE-RUM POUND CAKE (RECIPE, PAGE 189) INSTEAD OF THE FROZEN POUND CAKE.

APPLE DUMPLINGS

prep: 30 minutes / bake: 1 hour / serves 8

2 cups all-purpose flour
1 teaspoon salt
⅔ cup unsalted butter
¼ cup ice water
1½ cups sugar
1¾ teaspoons ground cinnamon
2 cups water
3 tablespoons unsalted butter
2 teaspoons shredded lemon zest
1½ teaspoons vanilla extract
2 tart cooking apples (such as Granny Smith), peeled, cored, and quartered
¼ cup (½ stick) unsalted butter
Whipped cream (optional)

1. Preheat oven to 350°F. In a bowl stir together flour and salt. Using a pastry blender or fork, cut in the ⅔ cup butter until the pieces are the size of giant peas. Sprinkle 1 tablespoon of the ice water over part of the flour mixture; toss with a fork. Push moistened pastry to side of bowl. Repeat moistening flour mixture, using 1 tablespoon of the ice water at a time, until flour mixture is moistened. Gather dough with your fingers so it cleans the bowl. Shape into a ball. On a lightly floured surface, use your hands to slightly flatten pastry. Roll it from center to edges into a 20×10-inch rectangle about ⅛ inch thick. Cut into eight 5-inch squares.

2. In a small bowl combine ½ cup of the sugar and 1½ teaspoons of the cinnamon; set aside. For syrup, in a saucepan combine the 2 cups water, the remaining 1 cup sugar, the 3 tablespoons butter, the lemon zest, vanilla extract, and the remaining ¼ teaspoon cinnamon. Bring to a boil; cook for 3 minutes. Set aside.

3. Place an apple quarter, cavity side up, in the center of each pastry square. Sprinkle sugar-cinnamon mixture over apple quarters; dot each with some of the ¼ cup butter. Moisten edges of pastry squares with water. Bring opposite points of pastry up over each apple; seal. Place in a 13×9×2-inch baking dish. Pour syrup around dumplings.

4. Bake, uncovered, about 1 hour or until apples are tender and pastry is golden. To serve, transfer each dumpling to a dessert dish. Spoon syrup over dumplings. If desired, serve with whipped cream.

G'S GOTTA-BE-QUICK TIP: ----------------

FOR A REALLY QUICK DESSERT, USE A 15-OUNCE PACKAGE ROLLED, REFRIGERATED, UNBAKED PIECRUST (2 CRUSTS) INSTEAD OF THE MADE-FROM-SCRATCH PASTRY. ROLL EACH CRUST INTO A 10-INCH SQUARE. CUT EACH CRUST INTO FOUR 5-INCH SQUARES.

CHOCOLATE-PECAN PIE

prep: 15 minutes / bake: 45 minutes / serves 8

1   9-inch unbaked deep-dish
      pastry shell
⅔   cup dark cane syrup or
      dark-colored corn syrup
½   cup sugar
      Pinch salt
½   cup unsalted butter
4   eggs
¼   cup unbleached all-purpose flour
½   teaspoon vanilla extract
½   teaspoon almond extract
1   6-ounce package semisweet
      chocolate chips
1   cup pecan halves

1. Bring pastry shell to room temperature. Preheat oven to 350°F. For syrup, in a small saucepan combine cane syrup, sugar, and salt. Heat over medium heat until sugar is dissolved and mixture comes to a boil. Remove from heat. Stir in butter until melted. Set aside to cool slightly.

2. Meanwhile, in a large bowl whisk together eggs, flour, vanilla extract, and almond extract until smooth. Whisk warm syrup into the egg mixture, adding syrup in a slow, steady steam.

3. Spread chocolate pieces in the bottom of the pastry shell; cover with pecans. Pour egg mixture evenly over the pecans. To prevent overbrowning, cover edge of pie with foil. Bake about 25 minutes; remove foil. Bake for 20 to 25 minutes more or until a knife inserted near the center comes out clean. Cool on a wire rack. Cover and chill within 2 hours.

BUTTER CAKE WITH COCONUT ICING

prep: 20 minutes / stand: 30 minutes / bake: 30 minutes / serves 12

1   cup (2 sticks) unsalted butter
4   eggs
2¾ cups all-purpose flour
2   teaspoons baking powder
1   teaspoon salt
½   cup milk
¼   cup sweetened condensed milk
¼   cup pineapple juice
1¾ cups granulated sugar
1   teaspoon vanilla extract
    Coconut Icing
½   cup flaked coconut

1. Allow butter and eggs to stand at room temperature for 30 minutes. Grease and flour two 9×1½-inch cake pans; set aside. In a bowl stir together flour, baking powder, and salt; set aside. In another bowl combine milk, sweetened condensed milk, and pineapple juice; set aside.

2. Preheat oven to 375°F. In a mixing bowl beat butter with an electric mixer on medium to high speed for 30 seconds. Gradually add granulated sugar, beating until well mixed. Beat 2 minutes more. Add eggs, one at a time, beating well after each addition. Beat in vanilla extract. Alternately add flour mixture and milk mixture, beating on low speed after each addition just until combined. Spread batter into prepared pans.

3. Bake for 30 to 35 minutes or until a wooden toothpick inserted near centers comes out clean. Cool cake layers in pans on wire racks for 10 minutes. Remove layers from pans; cool thoroughly on wire racks. Frost the top of one cake layer with Coconut Icing. Stack remaining layer on top. Frost top and side of cake. Sprinkle coconut on top of cake.

COCONUT ICING: In a mixing bowl beat 2 cups powdered sugar; one 8-ounce package cream cheese, softened; 2 tablespoons cream of coconut, and 1 teaspoon vanilla extract with an electric mixer on medium speed until smooth. Stir in ½ cup coconut.

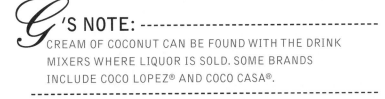

G'S NOTE: ------------------------------------
CREAM OF COCONUT CAN BE FOUND WITH THE DRINK
MIXERS WHERE LIQUOR IS SOLD. SOME BRANDS
INCLUDE COCO LOPEZ® AND COCO CASA®.

REMEMBER WHEN?

Since my first book *Turn Up the Heat* came out, I've realized something very special, and that's the power of support from my family and friends. But what's just as interesting is the love and support from people that I don't know, sometimes complete strangers. As I make my way through the airport, heading to do a cooking demo or an appearance, I get to meet an amazing number of people who truly care about what I do. These encounters help me understand that I am truly blessed to have the opportunity to do the one thing that I truly love—to cook.

I admit that going through the business of TV shows, book deals, branding, and all that comes with the life of a TV person can be stressful. I sometimes forget to let go and remember the time when none of this existed. I now have an opportunity to see the world. I have the freedom to speak, to reach out, and to teach through my love of food. I have the opportunity to meet people whose lives I've changed because of my book or my TV show. I have the chance to be reminded of the fact that there are a great many people who would love to be where I am. I've learned that there is a sense of pride, strength, and patience that I must always have. But I've also learned that I am not always right and that we all have to meet at the halfway mark sometimes.

I've been reminded to love and let go and take a look at the life that I may have made for myself but not by myself. I was once just a boy with a dream. Now I'm a man with a dream come true. So I try to remember the feelings of others, remember the work of others, remember the struggles of others. Others may not be as strong as me, so it's my job to protect them. And though I may not always agree, it doesn't make them wrong and it doesn't mean that we're not on the same side. As I say to myself and share with you, take pride in your accomplishments and your work, take ownership in your mistakes and faults, and take time to be sure that the people around you know that they are truly appreciated. When life seems complicated and overwhelming, remember the simple times and wonderful places that you might not otherwise ever think about. We call those moments "the good old days."

BLESSINGS,

GLOSSARY—WHAT YOU NEED TO KNOW

MAKE IT SUPER SIMPLE BY LEARNING A FEW BASICS, LIKE HOW TO DREDGE MEAT OR SMASH A GARLIC CLOVE. HERE ARE TECHNIQUES G USES IN HIS RECIPES THAT WILL HELP YOU BECOME A BETTER COOK.

AL DENTE—Literally "to the tooth," though it refers to cooking pasta or other food just until it still gives some resistance when bitten into, but is not soft.

BEAT—To make a mixture smooth by briskly whipping or stirring with a spoon, fork, wire whisk, rotary beater, or electric mixer.

BIAS-SLICE—To slice food, such as carrots, diagonally for a more attractive appearance.

BOIL—To cook food in liquid at a temperature that causes bubbles to form and rise in a steady pattern, breaking at the surface. A rolling boil occurs when liquid is boiling so vigorously that the bubbles can't be stirred down.

BROWN—To cook a food in a skillet, broiler, or oven to add flavor and aroma and develop a rich, desirable color.

CREAM—To beat a fat, such as butter or shortening, either alone or with sugar to a light, fluffy consistency. It may be done by hand with a wooden spoon or with an electric mixer. This process incorporates air into the fat so baked products have a lighter texture and better volume.

DREDGE—To coat food, either before or after cooking, with a dry ingredient, such as flour, cornmeal, or sugar.

DRIZZLE—To randomly pour a liquid, such as powdered sugar icing, in a thin stream over food.

EGG WASH—A mixture of egg and water or milk beaten together. This mixture is brushed on bread or pastry to create a golden color when baked.

FINISH—To add butter or cream at the end of cooking to give a dish added shine and richness.

GARNISH—To add visual appeal to a finished dish.

GRILL PAN—A skillet with raised ridges on its surface used on the stovetop to simulate outdoor grilling.

ICE BATH—A bowl of ice and water used to cool foods quickly.

IMMERSION BLENDER—A handheld wand blender with the motor at the top and a rotating blade at the bottom. Immerse the blade end of the immersion blender into a soup or other cooked mixture and blend right in the cooking pot.

MARINATE—To soak food in a marinade. When marinating food do not use a metal container, which can react with acidic ingredients and adversely affect food's flavor. Always marinate food in the refrigerator, never on the kitchen counter. To reduce cleanup, contain the food you are marinating in a plastic bag set in a bowl or dish. Discard leftover marinade that has come in contact with raw meat. Or if it's to be used on cooked meat, bring the leftover marinade to a rolling boil for 5 minutes before using to destroy any bacteria that may be present.

MINCE—To chop food into tiny irregular pieces.

PLATE–To arrange food on a serving plate in an attractive, appetizing way.

RENDER–To cook fatty meat over low heat so the fat melts and separates from the meat and the meat turns brown and crisp.

SAUTÉ– From the French word sauter, meaning "to jump." Sautéed food is cooked and stirred in a small amount of fat over fairly high heat in an open, shallow pan. Food cut into uniform pieces sautés best.

SEAR–To brown a food, usually meat, quickly on all sides using high heat. This helps seal in the juices and may be done in the oven, under a broiler, or on top of the range.

SEASON–To sprinkle foods with seasonings, such as salt and pepper, to improve their taste.

SHINGLE– To arrange food in a slightly overlapping pattern.

SMASH–To mash a garlic clove by pressing the heel of your hand on the flat side of a broad-bladed knife that rests on the clove.

SIMMER–To cook food in liquid that is kept just below the boiling point; a liquid is simmering when a few bubbles form slowly and burst just before they reach the surface.

STEAM–To cook a food in the vapor given off by boiling water.

SWEAT–To cook vegetables in a small amount of fat over low heat until they become tender and translucent, but not brown.

TENT–To loosely cover cooked meat with foil, like a tent, to keep the food warm while it continues to cook from the residual heat.

WHIP–To beat food lightly and rapidly using a wire whisk, rotary beater, or electric mixer to incorporate air and increase the food's volume.

WHISK–To use a wire whisk to combine ingredients.

ZEST–The colored outside part of a citrus peel, not including the bitter white part underneath. Use a fine shredder to remove the zest from citrus to add bright citrus aroma and flavor to food.

SHINGLE, PAGE 56

DREDGE, PAGE 74

SMASH, PAGE 31

EGG WASH, PAGE 19

INDEX

Boldfaced page numbers indicate photographs.

THE PREMIER
LIFESTYLE & ENTERTAINMENT
NETWORK FOR AFRICAN AMERICAN ADULTS